A WILD SURMISE

Also by Eloise Klein Healy

Building Some Changes

A Packet Beating Like a Heart

Ordinary Wisdom

Artemis in Echo Park

Women's Studies Chronicles

Passing

The Islands Project: Poems for Sappho

A WILD SURMISE

NEW & SELECTED POEMS
& RECORDINGS

for Raphe,

ELOISE KLEIN HEALY

Eloise Klein Healy
2013
Poet Laureate LA

RED HEN PRESS | *Pasadena, CA*

Book design and layout by David Rose

Library of Congress Cataloging-in-Publication Data

Healy, Eloise Klein.
  A wild surmise : new & selected poems & recordings
  / Eloise Klein Healy.—1st ed.
    p. cm.
  ISBN 978-1-59709-759-8
  I. Title.
  PS3558.E234W55 2013
  811'.54—dc23

                    2012030769

The Los Angeles County Arts Commission, the National Endowment for
the Arts, the City of Pasadena Cultural Affairs Division, the Los Angeles
Department of Cultural Affairs, the Dwight Stuart Youth Fund, and Sony
Pictures Entertainment partially support Red Hen Press.

First Edition
Published by Red Hen Press
www.redhen.org

Acknowledgments

I would like to thank the editors who originally published the new, selected, and uncollected poems, some in slightly different versions, in *Askew, Audemus, Bear Flag Republic: Prose Poems From California, Black Clock, BLOOM, Chance of a Ghost: An Anthology of Contemporary Ghost Poems, Chickasaw Plum, Electronic Poetry Review, Feminist Studies, Gertrude, Lambda Book Review Literary Spotlight, The Los Angeles Review, Matrifocus: Cross Quarterly for the Goddess Woman, Ms. Magazine, Poetic Dialogue Project, poeticdiversity.org, poetrymagazine.com, Prairie Schooner, RATTLE, The Rattling Wall,* and *The Women's Review of Books.*

• "Recipe With Dogs" was included in Terry Wolverton's Writers At Work *What's Cookin' Postcard Project.*

• "Mr. Twister" was written for Susan Silton's *The Tornado Project.*

• "At the Altar of the Peregrine" was written for display at Chan Chich Lodge, Belize.

• "The Summer She Died" was written for *Other People's Memories/ Found Photos: A Dialogue with the Anonymous,* an exhibit curated by Paula Gray at the Mendocino College Art Gallery.

Offering gratitude is an important part of putting together a book such as this one—new poems, poems selected from previous collections, and poems that for one reason or another never got into my other books. These poems all share one thing besides me having written them—another person cared about them, listened to them with me, read them, or heard them at a reading or on the radio. I didn't write any of these poems just for myself. They are all public acts; they were meant to live in the world. Many years ago, May Swenson told me that poems are perceptions, and it is true that my poems reflect and replicate mine. Many poems started because of a "*what if?*" proposition and I followed those leads.

I have been fortunate to live in a vibrant poetry community in Los Angeles, though we have definitely been under the radar much of the time. Thankfully, amazing editors and publishers chose to put my work in print or in digital format, and I am grateful to them every day of my life. Early on, I won a first book prize, The Beyond Baroque Foundation's NewBook Award for *Building Some Changes.* James

Krusoe was my editor and he taught me how to put a book together. *A Packet Beating Like a Heart*, under the editorship of Jacqueline De Angelis and Aleida Rodriguez, was the first poetry collection published by Books of a Feather Press. *Ordinary Wisdom*, a limited edition letterpress book, was handset and printed by Susan King of Paradise Press at The Woman's Building in Los Angeles (later reprinted by Red Hen Press). Nancy Bereano published *Artemis in Echo Park* at Firebrand Books, one of the first lesbian feminist publishing houses in the country. My chapbook, *Women's Studies Chronicles*, was part of the Illuminati Press's Laguna Poets Series (#99), published by Pat and Marcia Cohee. Kate Gale and Mark Cull of Red Hen Press published *Passing*, *The Islands Project: Poems for Sappho*, and now this book, *A Wild Surmise: New & Selected Poems & Recordings*.

There's an important underlying story here beyond my own publishing history—the growth and importance of independent publishing in American letters from the mid-twentieth century onward.

I began my work as a poet at a time when the poetry reading was a fairly new venue for interaction between poet and audience. It was also a time when the production of books and their distribution was opening up to a new kind of publisher. The Women's Movement had also begun to challenge accepted notions of what and who should be published, just as The Civil Rights Movement had directly and indirectly raised the question of who is allowed to create culture. Many people took the issue into their own hands, and my publication history is the result of these trailblazing efforts.

I regret that my parents did not live to see *A Wild Surmise*, though I know they often saw me as their own wild surmise. I am the happy offspring of a father who liked nothing more than taking things apart and putting them back together (or blowing them up!) and a mother whose language was wildly metaphorical and spoken in the cadence of conversations she presided over in her café. Bless them for everything. I have had a fortunate life.

I want to thank my friends in the MFA in Creative Writing Program at Antioch University Los Angeles, my poetry pals from the Idyllwild Summer Poetry Festival days, my sisters from The Woman's Building, the Red Hen staff, all the Arktoi authors, the Arktoi Advisory Group, and our first publicist, Nickole Brown. I remember and thank all my colleagues, students, and friends who have taught me how to be a human being, especially Joan Sears Sullivan. A big hug to my friend Tara Ison for her generous help with Arktoi Books and our conversations about literature and the writer's life.

Because reading my poems in public has been such an important part of my life in poetry, I wanted to have an audio element in this "new and selected" collection. Special acknowledgment goes to Harlan Steinberger of Hen House Studios, who recorded the poems that make up "the recordings" element of this book, and warm thanks to Michael C. Ford, who served as my cheerleader during the recording sessions. Without the help of Liz Bradfield and Colleen Rooney, the set-up of the audio files and QR codes for the readings in the book would have pushed me over the edge.

Special gratitude goes to the amazing artist Sage Vaughn for the use of *Irish Girl* on the cover.

As always, I thank my animal companions for their love, compassion, and revelation of different ways of being and knowing.

And finally, pura vida to my loving "other" of over twenty-five years, Colleen Rooney. Being in the world with her is pure magic.

Recordings of the Poems

There has been much talk about what is going to be the fate of "the book" in this electronic age. Most speculation centers on getting the book into another "form" that is downloadable from the Internet from a variety of sources. The only certainty is that it is too soon to tell what the final outcome will be. It seems, however, that the book and its descendants are here to stay.

But how about putting elements of the electronic age into a book?

When it came time to think about what I could do with my new and selected poems collection—the book of it—I felt that using a current technology could enhance a book of poetry by putting a reading inside it. Not a compact disc tucked in a special fold of a book jacket or a plastic box, but "on" the page with the poem.

The current technology in question, the QR, or quick response code, a square of squiggles linked to a web address and read by a smart phone application, seemed the perfect answer. This lowly advertising device could be made to deliver the poem and the poet to the reader.

So, for however long this technology lasts, the QR codes in this book will maintain their links to poems recorded by me at Harlan Steinberger's Hen House Studios. The recordings can also be accessed at my website where they will stay as long as websites are around. (http://www.eloisekleinhealy.com)

What is probably temporary is this technology; what is likely a little more lasting is poetry itself.

One can find QR code readers to download onto a smart phone or other mobile electronic device from various websites and stores offering these applications online. Directions for their use are offered at these sites as well. There are many wild surmises in my book—please enjoy this one.

—Eloise Klein Healy
Los Angeles, CA
June 19, 2012

This book is for Kate Gale and Mark Cull

CONTENTS

NEW POEMS:
A WILD SURMISE

FOREWORD

We go back, Eloise and I. Far back. In 1978 I was on sabbatical with my family in Arcadia, California. My husband was doing research at Caltech. Arcadia was very pretty, very boring, and the most frighteningly white place I have ever been. Everybody was white except the gardeners. Somebody kindly told us we were one of just two Jewish families in Arcadia. Luckily, I had an escape route. Once a week I got in the car and drove south on the Pasadena Freeway to Venice, and went to the open mike sessions at Beyond Baroque, led with exquisite courtesy by Jim Krusoe.

Those sessions were never boring, always fun and quirky, sometimes inspiring and moving. Everybody wasn't white. Everybody wasn't William Blake or William Wordsworth or even William Carlos Williams. Some of us were moderately crazy. But everybody cared about poetry, their own and each other's. There was a feeling of community. And the women were taken as seriously as the men.

What I remember most about Eloise in those Beyond Baroque days was her voice, flat-accented Midwestern, never apparently agitated, a voice that knew about work, a voice with a matte surface and brass undertones, a voice that always seemed able to have the last word because it was steered by common sense, insight, and a lot of human decency. She didn't dress up. She dressed like a boy. Her sense of humor tended to be poker-faced, with occasional wild smiles flaring up. She was easy to be with, for someone as shy as I was then. Best of all, she wrote poetry that locked onto reality.

During those years of turbulent feminism in America, Eloise was a major inspiration of the awesome Los Angeles Woman's Building. As founding chair of the Creative Writing MFA Program at Antioch University Los Angeles from 1997 to 2004, Eloise made sure that the program addressed issues of race, class, sex, and gender in America. As the century turned, her passion for the natural world led to trips with ECO-ARTS, a venture she cofounded combining ecotourism and creativity for women—hike a rain forest in Costa Rica or Ecuador by day, write about it in the evening, was the brilliant drill. I wish I had been on one of those trips. Let me tell you, though, even just walking through any green space in the vicinity of Los Angeles with Eloise, and hearing her name the living things, is a blessing. In 2006 she established

Arktoi Books, an imprint with Red Hen Press specializing in the work of lesbian writers. Naturally she is a fan of the poet Sappho and of the goddess Artemis. Naturally she loves dogs, most recently Nikita, peppiest and jumpiest Portuguese Water Dog on the planet. Then there's her Chinese brush painting, reaching out to yet another culture. What I am trying to say is that Eloise Klein Healy is a woman of body and soul, of activism and meditation, of Los Angeles and Earth. In Yiddish, we call a person like her a mensch.

There is a trajectory in this book, like the curving paths Healy likes to trace through landscapes. The voice is uniquely her own, recognizable from the wise playfulness of her first book, *Building Some Changes*, which was chosen to be the initial publication of the Beyond Baroque Foundation's NewBook series, to the lyric poetry—conversational, comic, poignant—of *A Packet Beating Like a Heart*, to the more reflective and philosophical poems of her *Ordinary Wisdom*. She begins with a gift for shapely phrasing, fresh metaphor, humor, earthy practicality, and gently compassionate insight into the tribulations of love. Increasingly she places her explorations of personal feeling in environments that make the human drama the more resonant: the city of Los Angeles (she has appropriated cars and freeways as setting and metaphor as well as any American poet I know), mechanics (which doesn't frighten her—read the triumphal poem called "Changing the Oil"), the ethnic mix of urban life, the submerged force of nature inside and outside us, politics, philosophy, myth. *Artemis in Echo Park* is a book of wide scope and power, combining myth and the momentary. She knows there is "a trail even under asphalt" and "a city beneath the city" that "dances like a calavera in the ballroom of the dead." She gets cats and coyotes into the poems—ancient truth, to put it bluntly—to give us a little more of what we need to survive as humans.

Truth isn't necessarily nice. In *Women's Studies Chronicles* Healy's anger is aflame. In *Passing*, she wrestles with tragedy. "Louganis" is a beautiful sestina about beauty and HIV. "Latin from the Mass" is composed of delicate triplets about cancer, "a stranger with a spearlike scalpel / slicing off your breast"—and you realize "mass" in that title is a grim pun. You'd say the woman is all heart, except that her craft is so good. The poet's elegies are filled with joy's memory and power, her lust insists on the rights and rites of the body, her compassion insists on the details. Then there is a kind of pause, in which the poet meditates on her voice. Poetry and the invocation of Sappho become central images in *The Islands Project: Poems for Sappho*, alongside heart-stoppingly tender poems for her mother. Healy has always identified herself as a lesbian poet, and this is what lesbian poetry today does: it reaches out into family, community, politics, and the wide world. Healy's work will touch any reader for whom human warmth and wit are desirable characteristics in poetry. In "Hardscape," childhood at an auto repair shop

> . . . made me hanker for hard things,
> want to get outdoors first light, handle sticks
> and dead tires, bang old mufflers together
> and bam a ball peen hammer
> against a scrap of sheet metal behind the shop.
>
> It made me not want dolls and the demands
> of indoors—quiet in the parlor, quiet by the stove.
> It made me a woman of landscape and weather
> and suspicious of my place. Say it gave me
> a chrome handle to a different and difficult world.

Finally, something new happens in the "new poems" here. Call it wisdom. Call it serenity. Call it acceptance—what happens when Japanese poets write their *jisei*, or death poems, or when James Wright breaks into blossom. Healy, "Having Broken into Blossom," writes, "there is no against / just to and fro,"

> and where before I wondered
> what and why   now
> I shyly bend and blend
> into the sensible breeze

Or call it redemption, as Healy does in a poem where she speaks first as the scared schoolgirl listening to Sister Perpetua talk about The Last Judgment, and then as Lot's wife,

> redeemed when I turned
> and went back to Sodom,
> to the friends and neighbors
> I had lived among all my life.
> Nothing untoward happened except
> I didn't count myself among the fearful anymore.

Near the close of *A Wild Surmise*, the poet celebrates a twenty-year-long relationship with her lover, recalling their first surmise—"we knew that we would be / the wilderness and all that can be found there"—and how it has been realized. A later poem celebrates one of the poet's dogs: "you always smelled like sun, too, / Black sun, clean-black as the afterimage of a falling leaf." The poem is a sensuous elegy mixed with a spark of satire:

> This is what the catechism warned about,
> attachment to things other than god.
> Love of another body
> without distinction and with pure delight.

People, dogs, the earth: what Eloise Klein Healy has for them is love, and words to make the love ring true.

—Alicia Ostriker

A WILD SURMISE

FROM
BUILDING SOME CHANGES
1976

FURNISHING

I wonder what to hang over the bed.
You don't care, you don't look
at walls. It took me a long time
to understand that difference between us.

Every item in a room influences me,
every item tunes the air,
the air playing across objects
makes the room vibrate.
Anyone who thinks about atoms
will grant me this.
I am receptive to these envelopes
that rooms are
and when I pass from one room
to another it changes me.

You don't tune in to this frequency
unless I ask you what
you would like to see
on the wall over the bed.
You always answer, "I don't look
at the wall. Why don't you put something
you like." My answer is,
"You might see it while we're making love.
How would that affect you?" You answer,
"I won't see it unless I hit my head on it,
but you'll see it for sure."

Right, very right, I will see it
and it will affect me even if it doesn't hit me
on the head, it will be humming there
on the wall like a TV screen.

So, I asked you if you'd like a mural
which you won't see. I asked it
silently because I know
the answer.

This is our difference. I always ask
for more and more specifics
while you have already answered
to the general category.
When we see one of these exchanges
coming, we laugh. You like to play
them out. They are like the little
dramas constantly at work in your head.

I could paint a mural of the Monet lily pads
because you liked them at Tom's
but the room would shimmer too much
for me to sleep and the project is too big
anyway. My other choice is to hang
Bosch's 'Garden of Earthly Delights'
over the bed. I hesitate
because the panels are difficult
to hang straight and I can imagine getting
very lost in those scenes.

Maybe if I saw them while making love
I would get stuck in the picture
or take it out of the frame
and impose it on you.

I am also afraid I might hit my head
on it. I know how often I am afraid of hitting
my head, even though I have never

seriously injured it.
When the football drilled me between the eyes
and broke my glasses
I watched it all the way.

I watched so hard I couldn't feel
the fear, everything got too slow
for fear. The football kept coming
in a perfect arc, I saw more and more
of the grain, the raised bumps—some brown
some white, then the point where all the panels
meet was spinning like a star and everybody
was yelling.
I'm sure I smiled just before it hit.

I think if I hung the Bosch over the bed
I would fall into it. I would hit my head
on the dancers' knees just like the time
I fell in basketball. Barbara's knee
came up at me very slowly. I thought
"Here it comes again, I'm going to hurt
my head." But I was not afraid, really,
only for my glasses.
It was the second pair I broke that year
and I was getting small scars
on the bridge of my nose.

I have seen things coming at my head
like this. I have been transfixed, watching
the object arriving like a cow at slaughter watching
the mallet descend, but judging, judging all the way.
I have seen the pieces of an action
slowly coalesce and grind to a halt

like the plates of California locking
far off underground months before a quake.

I wonder about hanging anything
over the bed in California
because of a mosaic that came down
last time.

I don't know how long I could hold off
the fear of a mosaic hitting me.
Maybe we'll be moving next year anyway,
so I won't hang anything
over the bed just now.

Storing Things

You talk about film kept
in the refrigerator since 1952.

I remember dinosaur bones disappearing
in the sun, have heard the succulent thump
of leaf falling upon leaf
and the churn of mold going to work.

Nothing keeps.
Everything is taken to pieces.
Earth is like a 17 year old boy
tearing down engines
for parts.

Minor Leagues

More trouble keeping
mildew out of the glove

than the farm-boy runner
at 2nd

who thinks there's no pickoff sign
he's missing.

Los Angeles

Like an older sister who wasn't quite as pretty
you were never expected to become much,
only to settle your larger body into the practicality
of middle age.
You were never expected to be charming
like the younger one
who could enchant.
There was something about your proportions
that was indelicate—your more abundant waist.
She always had the poetic suitors who
came to visit.
You always opened the door.

Nobody expected it
and you never told about
the lover who met you
loose and large
in the late afternoon
and loved you all night,
completely out of proportion.

The Pope at 7:00 p.m.

Does the Pope sit alone
with a china plate of spumoni
and a glass of white wine?

When it is all quiet
from theology,
does he read humility reports
from Mother Superiors
or check the scholastic progress
of native clergy from African places?

Does the Pope think on charity
and decide to give away
what the Vatican reaps?
At 7:15 does he think
of the library's collection
of pornographic literature?
Does he wonder if he could
give it away?

Does he ever eat too much
lasagna or spill
sauce on his small white shoes?

At 7:45 does he want to get undressed?
Does the Pope have pajamas,
a nightshirt, or nothing?
If he's sleepy, does he nod
and tip his glass
or must he read to fall asleep?

Does he read in American or Latin,
or does he have a clock alarm
from somebody as a present?
Or a television—
does the Pope know
the *Dating Game*?
Or does he just sit
there in the quiet
wondering what other people do?

Please Forgive Me

Please forgive me.
Think of me as a world
reduced to a map.

What I have had to flatten
and alter
to be understood.

Each new explorer has claimed
a boundary and gone home
without ever traveling my heartland.

They have measured me
for plunder
and changed my faith.

Is it any wonder
why I go on
accurately misrepresenting?

READING WHILE HAVING A SPRAINED BACK

The back sits straight. It is afternoon
and light fades like British lawns, away away
from the eyes to the fairy glens. The Druids come
out of a story and encircle.

The back has pain. Sprain is a container
of pain. The "r" stirs roughly and guttural
ridges run through the pain. The back moves.
The Druids rustle in the leaves. The page
is turned and the back moves again.

The sprain breathes in and out. The back
anticipates, tightens. The lawn closes and the Druids
of the pages like cardboard dolls fold inward.
The back and the sprain compromise. The sprain
slightly wins.

Snow Pack Café

for Clare

The sign on #395 remains legible,
broken neon tubing and faded paint
spelling out another failed enterprise:

Snow Pack Café.

Strangely lost in the middle
of the Mojave Desert,

it fronts a hot long highway slashing north to Reno,

the spine of the Sierra Nevada twisting
through every conceivable shade
of dry brown
behind it.

Yet I can believe an insistent stab of wind
pinned somebody's collar to neck,

widened the imagination's eye to admire
that hard, white speck with a death-grip handhold

hovering at 8,000 feet.

My Knees in a Love Poem

My mother warned me.
She worried
bruises looked terrible,
wouldn't go away.

I've done OK by my knees,
spotted wingtips of a butterfly
closing, like breaths,
around your head.

WHAT IS BEING FORGOTTEN

Quickly. What is being forgotten? Shirts
on a line with stiff arms. Dampening bottles
with cork-rimmed lids. Rain water heated
and sprinkled on white shirts. The wooden
legs of the ironing board and the iron heating.
Air like hot bread. Shirts flattening
under the iron. That every shirt needed
ironing is being forgotten.

A PACKET BEATING
LIKE A HEART

1981

AFTER THE LAST CALL HOME

which of our visions will claim us
which will we claim?
—Adrienne Rich, "Nights & Days"

I want to roll my life back
and find the way I played
with Tiny and Big Boy and Carol.
I want to roll my knuckles
down onto dirt
packed hard by tamping,
by marbles rolling,
in some games
a free hand leaning and pressing
as I was playing with friends
and we were playing "for keeps forever."

Then each day clicked against the others
like marbles in a bag,
each a favorite for its own reason
and each as pretty as a pony's eye.

It was so simple then,
writing with a stick on the ground,
drawing circles for clean hard games
that filled each moment
with happy predictability
and lasted until dark.

It's not so simple for me now.
Lines I write draw back into me.
Like furrows they break open
my familiar ground
to the awesome landscapes
of a female future

rising up inside me
with its fields that hold the horizon open
to I know I don't know what.

I want to roll my feelings back
to wandering the days
against all warnings
not to walk out in the corn
where I might get lost and never found
or be stolen by the gypsies
or eaten by a tiger
loose from a circus train.

I want to remember
the nights we stayed outside
against all warnings
and played in the dark,
buoyant with a sureness
taken in like air for a deep dive,
the nights I stayed out in the darkness
after the last call home
playing
what my life wants
to speak over and over again:

I'm not lost and I'm not leaving.
I'm out here in the night
with all the planets
in their deep rings of darkness
playing "for keeps forever" in the sky.
I'm out here in the invisible gravity
of my heartbeat
practicing the distances in me.

I'm drawing gypsy circles for myself
and leaping tigers through them
as high as I can go.

I Live in the City of Los Angeles

I live in the city of Los Angeles
where kids slide down
squat green hills
and women wind up Westerly Terrace
balancing on their heads
plastic baskets full of sheets
in dreamy bluewhite piles.

We are all from the country still
and we are each old
in our own way.

We are each old
from what we have seen.
We all have a little slow of handling,
a little smudge of coin color,
a little urban bruise.

We are all each old
from the sirens
and the guns
and the gaudy patter of the news,
from the totems of the gangs
and the choppers growling up the sky.

We bear the climate's lazy force
behind glasses all day
like conquistadores
snapping their helmets
against the sun,

against the light that leans hard
and borrows all the colors from our clothes,
then gives them back
to neon and the night.

It's the same light
that in the late afternoon
stutters when the doors open
and ribbons itself out on the rug,
stopping for a minute on this side of town,
stopping for a minute to say one more thing.

DARK

I'll tell you why I'm afraid of the dark.
It has its own idea.
It's like a bullet.
It doesn't want to know what you know.

The dark is under.
It fits a place to put a hand but I can't see.
It's like a voice behind a door.
It can be just about anything I want to hear.

Darkness comes in every size of threat:
the dark cocoon at the end of my life,
storms that turn the sky into an empty can of dark
fitting snug onto the horizon,
the dark in putting my head in hands,
my head into the cave of a person I don't love anymore.

I'll tell you again why I'm afraid of the dark.
I can see it coming
and can't ever tell just when it has arrived.
I sense it thin and waiting between the pages of books
but it's too fast even for a good reader.

From that place darkness
comes a phone call erratic with grief.
It fills the story called "dying in your sleep"
and was the only time left for voodoo to take,
for rapists to dress in.

I can't get a grip on darkness
though it wears my imagination like a shroud.
I've started hearing sunsets as cracking twigs.
I've taken to hiding a piece of flint in my shoe.

A Mile Out of Town

The Golden Pheasant was the Travelleer,
was the Red Star before that,
was the place my mother tended bar
and managed the motel,
was the corner my dad owned
the garage and gas station.

One orange night lard caught fire
and burned the Red Star out of our lives,
burned the illegal punch boards
and the prizes stacked under the counter,
burned through grease soaked floors
and blacked all the hamburger buns stacked
in white cellophane boxes.

So we moved from the trailer
into the new motel and lived in the big unit,
the one next to the fuzzing neon sign
that flashed VACANCY or NO VACANCY
through the nights.
I learned to ride a bike there
in our front yard of red rock chips,
fishtailing and skidding with my mother
alongside to steady the turns.

And we had a new place to work, the Travelleer.
Pine and sheet rock shingle siding and a red roof.
I told my mother goodnight there many times
behind the thick high bar, pushing my way
through the grownups who hugged and gave me
whisky kisses. There was always a half-breed dog
to follow me home.

Before I was in first grade I was tall enough
to look into the soapy dishwater,
could dry glasses and make them squeak,
could cut French Fries with my dad and lift
them in wire baskets out of the hot fat.
When we worked in the kitchen it meant Cook
was drunk, but he was a good cook and told me
stories, his cigarette sticking to his lip.
He had the only tattoo I'd ever seen and I guessed
it must have come from the Navy.

The weekends were dance music and cars
turning in from the highway late at night,
people puking in the parking lot, men standing
by pickups talking and laughing with women,
June bugs in the summer frying themselves
on the neon.

We made beds and beds and beds
for accordion players, organ players
and sometimes a three piece band.

I mostly played alone,
was Gene Autry and Roy Rogers,
a football player in white sandals,
a paratrooper jumping off combines and corn pickers
with a Blo-Up life vest for a chute.
I begged my mother for guns and holsters,
rifles and footballs. She thought something was wrong
with me, I never pretended to be a girl
or wanted to dress that way.
I imagined skirts into fantasy ritual items
and wore hats to church as tribal garb.

Levis were all I wanted and I wore them
like a biker until the dye made my legs blue.

I hurried among adults, mumbling
like a radio left on low,
a running, bedraggled pygmy in loose curls,
armed with sticks, old pans, a motley uniform
of pinafore top, brown oxfords, a red cowboy hat
and a coaster wagon, all of it beginning to be a poet,
talking to itself.

And every year on the feast of St. Nicholas
out of nowhere candy flew
through the window, the expected fruit of believing,
of being rooted there, growing up a mile from Remsen, Iowa,
on the two lane highway
with the tall green corn all around.

THIS DARKNIGHT SPEED

Sometimes I feel about love
like driving places at darknight speed
with the radio on,
doing what that saxophone
was barking in the bar:
"better yet, better yet, better get in a car!"

Sometimes I forget
simple words like rapture
for this animal joy,
this sense of being up to speed
and merging from a ramp,
knowing the driver in the mirror
is already adjusting to meet me
and wants it to go smooth,
wants me to have my turn,
not break acceleration
or miss a beat,

wants to meet and make a dance of it
at such a speed,
if you can imagine,
at such a speed that eyes tear from wind
blowing music out the windows.

I always believe
I could start pacing with somebody
on a long highway,
playing all the fast songs
and looking at the truck stops
for that one car

because sometimes I'm lonely
or I need to feel alive
or I just like being on the road in a car,
in a marvelous, monstrous killer machine
that fills a human body crazy high
on landscape flying by the windows—
just a blur, just a shot of speed.

I always believe
I could get myself in somebody's eyes
wide and interstate-steady,
just flat out speeding along
and scanning the road ahead,
wanting to drive
like that
forever

and if I could keep it up,
god, if I could keep that up

I'd go absolutely right straight crazy to heaven

A Packet Beating Like a Heart

While in the employ of the reigning environment
among small cornered shopping centers
and a tangled tangle of straight lines
across the floor of a former beanfield
called the San Fernando Valley

I chanced to come upon a packet
wrapped in scented remembrancers
and a ribbon that was woven of glass, I'm sure,
or the lucid memory snapping clear in focus of colors
imagined while reading a story.

And the packet was beating like a heart, I swear,
or the memory I have of colored diagrams of hearts
opening and closing their little doors endlessly,
one door opening and one door closing and on and on.

My world meanwhile was filling up with afternoons
and the packet's beating and I had my eye on the traffic
I imagined myself entering
while the ribbon on the packet came loose
with ordinary handling, in the normal course of events,
because it was what was next as things go,
the packet opening itself out to reveal

a fable wrapped inside about a deer who lived in fear of death;
who everyday went to the shore of her small island
and watched the trees for the ravaging tigers of that place
until one day someone in a boat
shot her with an arrow from the sea and she fell.

I must say again that in the course of my employ,
quite by chance and not by plan, but like the best
of all accidental ventures, coming completely
out of the blue a packet beating like a heart
fell into my hands and thus I am the agent
of the tale I found written there on a paper
full of fine tigers that wrapped itself about
the story of a deer looking over her shoulder,
much like me in this as I was calling friends,
trying to make my way, planning pieces of the future
without regard to the shape of the present,
living on an island and hoping to find it Paradise
and conversely hoping to find that my way
is all the island I need because there is no shore then
to turn my foolish, frightened back on,

but there was a boat
and there was an arrow
and I have felt that little death of a single deer
in my life, my heart
opening open now to its story

WISDOM OR THE HUNGRY THING

for May Swenson

Wisdom.

You tried to show me
a young owl
hidden in the trees,
white as daylight,

a secret
night drifter,
dream deadly when dropping noiselessly
down,
talons arched and scything
above the grass,
then sinking into fur
and spine,
snapping shut like a watch face
closing up on time.

A bird of poetry,
young wisdom changes
its nest
to private heights
when too many footsteps
disturb its perch.

Not like the hungry thing
I feed—a jay,
the greedy one
who squawks and stamps,
screeches and yammers
even in the rain.

It comes here like poetry.
Poetry,
wings folded
in a blue dive
like a swimmer riding
a black wave inland.

It's a hungry thing
that will live in the back yard
close to food,
closer and closer to me,
approaching me raucous
with its right to be fed,
approaching me hungry
to store away
more than two birds could eat.

But still it's blue wing
I admire most
and legs like lacquered sticks
quick upon my porch.

Noisy coming right at me,
not hidden in daylight,
but made of daylight
and two slashes of nightfall
banding back from beak to eye,
two night-lined legs and claws
on which a blue hour dances
toward me,

a hungry noisy thing
everyday at my door
awaiting me
and my red robe,
its little sunrise
signal to swoop
and holler and demand more.

Poetry.

Wisdom
you tell me
keep looking for.

Poetry
the hungry thing
you tell me train and feed.

Poetry,
the hungry wisdom
demanding more,
flying down out of hiding
from a nest
in close trees,
flying in daylight
down out of the trees
looking for me,
demanding more to eat.

My Love Wants to Park

My love wants to park
in front of your house.

Thank God.
It's been driving me crazy
going around and around the block.

It's started breaking laws,
obsessively rolls through boulevard stops,
changes lanes without looking back.

It's taken over the transmission,
drops into second when I try to drive by
and rolls down its own windows.
I had to pull the horn wires
after it learned to "a-uugah"
at the sight of your address.

So just come out here please.
Please, just look under the hood
and kick the tires.

Try to stay away from the back seat.

DRIVEN TO MEET YOU IN RAINY WEATHER

Because there is so much wanting,
because desire is muscle and blood,
I wait for you in rainy weather
because my arms are full of life,
because the wind that flusters my umbrella
will shake your shining hair,
because metal posts and signs
can't warm to the beauty
of rain on your face like I do.
We are driven because of so much wanting.
We are driven muscle and blood
to hold and wear each other.
We are driven because the weather
in our veins is warmer than the world.

The weather in our veins
is warmer than the world
and as necessary as that storm was
to teach us to pass tools
across your muddy hillside,
to teach us we touched through work,
we touched through shovel handles,
tile pipe, the rocks we carried.
And wet all through and dirty and laughing
we stopped all the water
we could stop,
channeled it off in trenches
dug by hand,
saved what we could save
and I worked harder to reach you
than I knew.

I worked harder to reach you
than I knew.
Was it three years or twenty years
from turning my head from my feelings
and like the old cliché,
talking about the weather
but not being able to change it?
Don't blame yourself for what I feel.
I say blame the sky, blame clouds,
believe in the stars' grip of fate
or the power of the moon to pull tears
down my face.
But don't blame yourself alone
for the storm breaking inside me,
and don't ask me not to cry
when I think I could lose you now.

Don't ask me not to cry
when I think I could lose you now.
Too much has happened, too much
like all the rain this year
when one cloudburst followed another,
turned simple roads into rivers.
Don't ask me not to feel adrift.
The whole world this winter
was afloat, sudden and powerful
waterfalls roared out of the hills.
But that was nothing compared to loving
and loving finding you, finding myself
driving in water over my wheels,
driving to meet you in rainy weather.

ENTRIES: L.A. LOG

1

The stars shine all day
through my scalp
five foot three inches into space
called atmosphere
or one of the ways to understand a novel.

2

At this address
a bougainvillea lifts her curls
and kisses a Santa Ana with her mouth open
right on its blueblue skies.

3

I like to ride the fast lane,
es muy caliente
and under me a red chile siren
pepper peppers Alvarado with cop sauce
as I cross.

4

I know I know
I'm dying a little faster of Los Angeles
but I suck in a piece of it anyway,
sing it out in little puffs
LA LA LA LA
about twenty times altogether
like a bunch of cheerleaders
yelling down the freeway in a bus.

5

Coiling out to Malibu
on a copper strand,
my sunglasses shine
like two westbound storefronts
open to the scenery business.

6

I never owned a map
to the stars' homes
but I sent to JPL
for 8 x 10 glossies of Mars
to stick up around my mirror.

7

I note the traffic patterns
of two Western Gulls
flying the Santa Monica Freeway,
sooty boomerangs
arching across their backs
as they exit up.

I Spent the Day with You

I spent the day with you like a drunken sailor
wanting you tattooed inside my life,
drawn dark blue
as the memory of dangerous foreign cities
and intricate
as unimaginable promises
shore lights make from the deep.

You looked oceans into me,
and set loose upon those currents
like a Columbus I lied about the miles out
because all hands believed still
there was an edge
and the sails were full to it,
the seas were fast to it,
faster even than the lanes of air.

I shook to tell what shudder filled me
high to low as I went willingly
to the ends of my map for you,
living headfirst through every wave
like the figure of a wooden woman
spearing through the seas,
vibrating with equal force
to a sense of passage and a sense of arrival.

I glittered like an earring made of gold,
like a tale you alone would tell,
throbbing with oriental opulence,
where beaches curled around the turquoise coves
and every spice I saw you
I could smell.

So chose to keep the needle working
deep and deep,
such colors blooming through my skin:
a heart your name unfurls,
the red swell that aches,
this strange design
I bared my body to you for

THE WORDS "BEGIN AGAIN"

She said "I don't love you"
I heard "invent zero"
and all of me flew
in clots and scatters
like the fast facts of an exit wound
smearing the room
when a bullet passes through the brain.

There's no keeping that blood on a page.
It dries into words that cake and break
into dark brown chips
which all together again
don't know a thing about the empty place
that once had held them whole.

I became an empty circle
locked in place like the zero
that keeps positive and negative worlds apart
but does not count in either,
does not bounce like a comma between
that stops, then lets the sense begin again.

I read in Stein the words "begin again"
and have tried to move myself out of my familiar mirror
of a woman fallen in a frozen lake.
Each poem is me inching out across the ice
to save her, to hold and warm her,
to feel the filling and relaxing,
the receding and expanding
of my own self again
like a pond alive to every sway of moon.

And seeing now
the wild cats and kittens that cross my yard
and the spiders that set out each afternoon
through the tomato plants
I know that what she took from me
did subtract from these bright wonders
and left me with a bitter wish
that hope counts
from an empty place,
and only from an empty place
does hope begin again.

OH MY EMOTIONS THESE DAYS

Oh my emotions these days
like the bone dance
I ride
over the raised dots
changing lanes
following your car
down the coast highway
with the sea quiet
on its edge.
I have to warn you,
one of your taillights is broken
and I want you very much.

ORDINARY WISDOM

Dividing the Fields

Real boundaries run underground
or are swathed in place by moonlight.
Through the orchard garden
a strip of clay on the diagonal
makes more happen than the furrows
we so carefully pegged out
to catch the proper path of the sun.
And who told the Forest Service
the fire-break hits exactly
the right zone?
Nothing takes hold in that clay.

Plants would get most answers right
if left to themselves.
Seeds have good heads
given any luck at all.
And that moon tonight,
you watch it.
That moon and those trees
have worked together dividing things
since they were girls.

Exhalation

Paper I write on is already used on one side
by the time I get it.
Third hand from the tree, almost a breath,
a ghost of paper when I get it.
Full, it is used up.
Emptied, I am full.
Everything breathes out and back
and I should never buy paper
to work on.
Empty on one side
empties enough of me.
I should cook more dinners
and sing more songs.
Feed my friends
and make my guests laugh.
All my virtues look like virtues to me
when I fall into bed tired
and the food is all eaten
and my friends have gone home
happy.
Then I know the breath of how many flowers
I am worth.
Breathing out, breathing in.
Relationship of use,
empty and full.

STANDING UP, LOOKING IN

This country is preparing a war,
inking the insides of guns
to print the right death,
and I am on a hillside far away,
anxious the wind will blow me
face first into a tall yucca
I'm smelling today.

When I walk down by the highway,
strangers wave at me
and I wave at them when I drive past
road crews, survey crews, the telephone repair.
But the war will be popular again.
There are strangers to be against
and the irony is always missing.
We even marry strangers.

Here I stretch, I stand tall
and stick my nose close
to the sappy ooze of waxy white blossoms,
purpled edges, the open smell.
War has density and seriousness.
I have just my balance
and my tremendous desire to reach.

WATER

The pond has found a place to go
and remembers
water's oldest mind,
move downhill.
So takes the split
the oleander found
and trickles out the seam,
knows this is breath again
to push this whirl
around this leaf.
Find the lower place.
This is breath
to work side to side.
Wait for strength,
then further along
rushing open notes
split the world
and pour through.
In vain, the caretaker shakes his head,
tries plugging the leak with stones and mud.
Water, he says, you can't take small steps with it.

To Speak for Human Feelings

It's a dangerous feeling
to want to love and protect you
because I'll be human
that much longer.
I won't have to buy so many things
to be happy
and I'll be human that much more.

It's a dangerous gesture
to walk arm and arm with you
to the store
because I won't forget
where I came from—the need
for human touch,
and I'll be human
so much simpler
if it shows.

Every word I put on paper
is a shout against the distance
between us all,
and I'll be human
that much deeper
if my saying so
makes arms around your shoulders
and our silence come undone.

ARTEMIS IN ECHO PARK

1991

ARTEMIS IN ECHO PARK

I turn out the driveway, point down the street,
bend where the road bends and tip down the hill.
This is a trail even under asphalt.
Every street downtown cuts through adobe
and the concrete wears like the curve
of a bowl baking on a patio or the sway of a brick wall
drying in the sun.
The life before cement is ghosting up
through roadways that hooves and water
have worn into existence forever.
Out to Pasadena, the freeway still behaves
like a ravine, snaking through little valleys.
The newer roads exist in air, drifting skyward,
lifting off the landscape like dreams of the future.
We've named these roads for where they end—
Harbor Freeway, Ventura Freeway, Hollywood Freeway—
but now they all end in the sky.

THE REAL BEARS HAVE GONE NORTH

The real bears have gone north
and in their place are grizzlies
with modern noses and paws with thumbs
prowling the underbrush
of public parks and back alleys.
Once when they were sacred, the girls
went to the woods to live like bears
before becoming women. Wild for the weeks
of initiation, they slept in wooly piles
under the moon and sang the songs of bears.
Now at the grocery, wildlife roams up and down
between the cars, sniffing handouts from shoppers
and knowing better than to snap or bite.
One woman brings her own cub and maybe
the young of others. She's thin as a mongrel
and her baby's too young to hold out her own hand.
What countryside is this, what species
am I feeding with my loose change
and dollar bills like dry leaves I give them?
When I was a girl I had to pretend
the groves of trees were full of people.
Now the world is peopled enough
and in the middle of this tropical city
I imagine oaks, I imagine the land
could still feed us.

THE VALLEY OF THE AMAZONS

She went to the grocery store with me
in North Hollywood wearing a black tank top
and no bra. We stood together in line.
Everybody was looking at her breasts,
her aviator glasses, her hair slicked back
and one strand falling over her eyes.
I felt like we were in a clearing
ready to mount the horses.
The men stood at a distance.
Our nakedness was nonchalant, connected
to horses and skin warmth. We would ride off
when the checker tallied our purchases
and the clearing would smell like horses
the rest of the day.

I Live Where I Live

I live where I live because
it has nothing to do with me.
I could go on about the choices I've made
and all the other elements of my landscape,
emotionally carved or artfully decorated,
but the real truth is, here you can see
the ribs showing through.
The land's way eventually surfaces.
It's all softening like old chenille,
faint voices on patios in the summer nights.
So I say this has nothing to do with me
but it comes to my door
and I let it in. I have the conversation
I wouldn't have with Jehovah's Witnesses.
I have brandy. I cook a little red snapper.
I remember Mazatlan and the plants
taking over, turning over the pots,
covering walls. This has nothing to do with me,
this wildness that softens everything.
Then again, it has nothing to do but me.

TOLTECS

Radio about a foot-and-a-half
wide swinging at his side.
Three boys abreast and one
has the radio playing loud rock
they talk to as they walk
past my house. Three boys
dressed in their style
of short jackets and caps pulled
down almost to their eyes.
They might as well be naked
boys in the hot sun singing
in a changing boy voice the songs
they like to hear. They might
as well be boys chipping rocks
into weapons or tools.
But they are only boys on the way
someplace. They have to be men
sometime and no time for idle
rambling to rock music unless
they take jobs in the outdoors
where they can still be boys
and dress to get dirty. They can
be boys underneath the culture
forever because some other man
will gladly take those boys
and chip them down into tools
or weapons or bake them into
the walls of his own idea
of empire.

THE CITY BENEATH THE CITY

I own a print of cows on a green hill,
brown-and-white cows
like peaceful wooden cutouts
who dream me through the wall,
through my neighbor's house, straight back
to old Pasadena—Rancho San Pasqual,
Rancho Santa Anita, and the wild cows
with arching horns, their spines knobbed
and hairy, 3-D and mean.

Their hides, I know, became chairs a century ago,
the hair reddish brown and white wore smooth.
The extra hides shipped down to the harbor
were traded for furniture carted home
to the main house on the two-wheeled *carretas*
up the track that's now the Harbor Freeway
out the ravine to Pasadena.

Little black olives pocking the dust
were picked and pickled in brine.
In the *zanjas*, horses drank
and scum floated on the water
green as neon.
From los ranchos to Sonora,
young ladies traveled in society.
The population of Chinese workers
was kept small—no women allowed—but
under the Governor's mansion, while
his daughter gave piano recitals and sang,
the Chinese dug tunnels north
from Olvera Street where their wives would live
in hiding. Under the cover of night
they spread out the secret earth to dry.

Some days still the ground shivers, splits
open the face of an unmined seam.
The city beneath the city dances
like a *calavera* in the ballroom of the dead.
The old bones shake when a shovel
strikes an amber bottle
or excavations uncover stone canals
mysterious as the mountains on the moon.

The Peahens

River noise replacements have appeared.
Massive rumble of the freeway
in the afternoon. Truck going down
through its gears. Helicopter cutting a circle.
Across the street the black-and-white dotted
dog some call Daisy or Droopy or Bonnie
looks like a cow grazing on the steep lawn.
That's where the peahens stood so still
the day one of them walked in front
of a car. Her wings hushed in air
and whacked on the pavement
and a thick red river of blood pooled
like red tar on the asphalt.
Her sisters stood like frightened girls
or stone statues. They ignored the wake
of bread bits and birdseed I set out.
They didn't venture onto the street
much after that. Then someone shot one
from its perch. One was stolen. One's left.
I hear her calling over the rush of wind
in the avocado tree.

ARTEMIS

I am thinking about romance and its purpose.
Children and why I didn't have any.
I would have left the cave and them with it
or I would have tied them to me forever
with my own sad dreams and finicky order.

I've liked young animals better.
I could put their heads in my mouth.
I could lick and clean them like a mother,
but I could not raise a child.
The first thing a child should see
is the pink sunrise of a nipple, not the green wind
of a branch whipping in passing.

I chose to keep animals around me instead
because we are the same. We have habits
and make strange circles before we sleep.
We don't like to be watched while we eat.

This Place Named for Califia

If the sun weren't just now
setting or maybe it's the mist—
this season's late night and early
morning fog—you could see it
off the coast, simple as Catalina
but bejeweled as a barge on the Nile,
that island, floating like the legends
ahead of an exploring army.
The story of the women beyond
the river, the falls, or like this
place, the island of women
in this place, black Amazons
living without men just beyond
the mist, beyond this weather. Dazzling
as it rises, an island real enough
to be necessary, a kind of woman
necessary enough to be real.

UP TO TOPANGA

Up to Topanga the road cuts down
to the muscle, a sea-laid matrix
of rock and shell the creek carves through.
Full moon, the sea at my back
glazed dark blue.
There's a coyote in my headlights
with her inevitable smile.
Sweet dancer, she leaps the double line
and I climb higher, following your car.
The man who tried to pick you up
at dinner started a war in me.
I could have charged with furious tusks
in that underbrush of talk, but I kept it
where women like me keep things, quiet—
until later when you held me like a girl.
Eyes smiling like coyote, you changed
my jealousy into passion, threw your hair
over me like a coat of fur and into the forest
of the moon I chased you.

ANOTHER POET WRITES ABOUT LOVE

Another poet writes about love
and I'm puzzled.

It's out there for him
in what he calls a lady.

He says she touches him
lightly on the ribs,

but I'm sure it's just his idea
that's touched. Something's missing

in his conception of completion.
He wants her to bring it to him,

be Eve at nightfall coming home,
completing him with tenderness.

I have been with women enough to want
tenderness igniting, sending the ribs

out to their filled extension
and sparks of flame

down the dry tendrils of my arms.
I want to die and rise and never be

completed in tenderness.
I want to burn the covering plants

to the ground and mulch them under.
I want good black earth instead of love.

Cactus

In the nursery, I always go to the cactus first.
Who are they anyway? Old ghosts, perhaps,
who meet you on their own terms.
Then I leave them and walk into ferns, cooler
heads, and palms, long arms and secretive.
I circle. If this were love I'd be thinking
opposites attract because I'm back
at the cactus counter fixed on someone
called Goat's Head. But what did that poet say,

the one who was holding a woman so high
off the ground? Something about tenderness in love?
When I look at the cactus in my hand,
my hand carefully raising the green plastic cup,
I think love is the spines,
the spines that curve and radiate
in parallel lines.
Love is how close you can get and even bleed
and even want to pick it up again.

WHAT IT WAS LIKE THE NIGHT CARY GRANT DIED

Cary Grant was dying all that time
we took to talk about romance
and what little chance there is
to see on screen even the evening we spent,
talk and turn of events, how everything went
this way for the dyke singer and that way
for the queer star, and what a funny
type we are, so normal in our taste
for bliss, but then there's the way
we kiss, unseemly on the screen
to see so much between two women,
the queen card played upon the queen.

And Cary Grant was dying until dawn
the night we carried on and on
about romance, the chances in a glance,
the votes we cast for whom we've asked
into our hearts' open beds. What was it
Dietrich said? No more talkative alive
than dead, that one, and who's to blame
for her closed case, the gorgeous face
that couldn't change its straight facade.
It would have been too odd to see
a woman in a pair of pants begin
her dapper dandy dance. An audience
would have died from it—the fragile pair,
the dalliance, the slicked-back hair.

The King of Romance drifted off from Iowa
and Hollywood the night he was to say
what it was like for him. The night he died,
that night we came away from talking until dawn
about the scenes and sounds that don't go on
the screen in living color of what's between
a woman lover and her lover.

CHANGING THE OIL

I get her up on the curb, two wheels off the street
and dive under with my tools—my favorite blue-handled
wrench and a drop-forged hammer with a no-slip grip.

Her, her, her—always the female car. And now I'm under,
lying on the news of the day before yesterday, slowly turning
the warm nut. She's above me like a womb or heaven
about to rain. I'm slowly turning my way into her
black blood, slipping on the wet bolt, diving into
the underworld we women crawl into with our new pride
fresh from the parts store. Turning the beautiful
implements over in my hands, tenderly
the oil spurts free—and I have done it.

MOON ON THE PORCH

Moon on the porch thumps his tail when I climb
the stairs. He's got a rock in mouth, old dog,
and will I play? Old teeth worn into stubs
from carrying rocks. Old Moon who limps
as far as we'll walk him. Drinks from the hot
tub when you're not looking, when the moon slides
over the edge of the roof and naked into the water.
I didn't know then this would be a poem to all
my lovers, planted by you in the full moon,
the water running off your breasts, falling
like silver coins into a pool. I didn't know then
how many women I was learning to love.

The Concepts of Integrity and Closure in Poetry as I Believe They Relate to Sappho

1

There's always the question
what else or *what more.*
A fragment of papyrus,
a frame from a film.
Wholeness but no closure.
Just what you'd glimpse—
two women suddenly arm in arm
crossing the beach front walk,
the waves running like mares
behind them.

2

What is a month, for example?
Tear it out of a year like an eye
and what do you see?
Unimaginable to expect a year
could be missing an eye, or is it harder
to think of it
having one? Questions of parts
of what,
this is how I've felt trying
to look out of my self.
Just quick takes,
motor-driven and waiting for the day
it all makes sense.

3

Sappho is the lesson of parts.
Libraries you must do without
because you are the book.

4

This is what happens at parties
where women dance with one another.
Everyone kisses. Old lovers.
Tribes assume this.
Kiss and kiss. Just that much of that.
Book and book and book. I have been learned
by heart. Lovely Sappho taking in
a glance at a lovely thigh, flower
arranging someone's hair.
Like that.

Across the patio
in a canvas chair, you know
the living danger sitting there.
A fragmentary glance. An hour
in her arms, disarray
you carry for another hour
or a year, years from that day
you keep like a piece of mica or a negative.

I have held to my lips
for a moment things like smoke. Smoke
from a burning book.

5

The waves ran away like mares
and the silver sat in its soft cloth
and the shells of the sea rolled
and dragged lovingly up and back.
And some of those women simply saw
each other and some of them saw
the sea.

But Sappho, she saw everything.

WILD MOTHERS

Wild kitty sneaks up my stairs
with two wisps of tiger behind her.
Wild mothers always find me.
Red Tail who lived in my driveway
and that chew-eared thing
who grew old in my carport.
Three bowls of dry food
every day and their tribes
in proscribed circles
waiting for me.
One-legged Scrub Jay waiting, too.
Lost ocelot hiding in the garage,
escaped cockatoo raucous in the eucalyptus.
Sparrow nesting over my doorway.
Mockingbird in the wisteria.
They find me where the clearing meets
the trees and night and light cross.
I have needed that they weren't mine,
that they would only come that close.

THIS ART, YOUR LIFE

The MRI scan reads a tumor in your brain
about the size of an eraser on a pencil,
but what space is it sharing, what room
does it take up, what does it push
aside as it reaches for your optic nerve,
threatening first your color sense, then vision?

I remember you walking to my cabin, a vision
appearing out of nowhere, blowing my brain-
bound sense of rules, operating on nerve
instead, kissing me first, then taking pencil
and paper to sketch the sunlit hills, push
against nightfall and my little room's

lack of light. In bed, there was barely room
to turn over, a small single, but vision
from a larger world was about to push
me past all limits, past what my brain
could handle, our bodies flying, pencil
line strands of hair electric as a nerve

network alight and glowing, each nerve
firing, drawing forth the spirit of the room,
transformed now by our loving. No pencil
sketch, no charcoal smudge, but fiery vision
of what women find and give beyond the brain-
washed fractured ways we've had to push

through to create selves in ourselves, to push
into our books, our paintings—this nerve
of being that shoots straight into the brain,
changing every pathway like arranging room
after room in your house to suit your vision

of space, of light, of how right it was in pencil
drawings. But know each time any pencil
fits into your grip, I wonder as you push
the sketch to fit the scheme of your vision,
are you safe enough? How can I calm you, nervous
as I am, take you into the room
of my heart and keep you from harm? It's brain-

less hoping for such power. Take pencil. Brain
storm again. Life is what we push for. Make room
for daily dogged vision. Then, live on nerve.

FROM

WOMEN'S STUDIES
CHRONICLES
1998

Intro to Women's Studies

They sit like a grove of saplings or young angels,
unmindful of how their faces are open to me,
how every line so lightly carving their brows
is familiar, how their eyes betray what they're hiding
from me, from each other, from themselves,
even the walls of the room.

Strewn in chairs or at attention, they wait,
hoping to add the class, maybe willing to behave
and sit like proper domesticated animals,
read all the books and turn in papers with no excuses.

This power to give life or take it
is what the avenging goddess must have felt,
but for me now it's reduced to
giving credit.

The young women hold everything in check,
the men measure me and before
the week is out, one or two will offer up
reductively sexist statements
to see if the hair on my spine will stiffen.
Yes, and then I will bite, maul, tell the truth
and tell it in terms they know.

The avenging goddess would have welcomed
the same kind of offerings—the great pile of shredded
animals burned to Artemis, bulls and goats torn
limb from limb and hanging on the ceremonial trees.
Yes, the goddess understood how far
the knife must go, the sacrifice must hurt,
to change the world.

I say to the women
 you will have powerful feelings,
 will fight with parents and boyfriends,
 will remember you have been raped or abused,
 will have to move away from home,
 maybe quit your job, change everything
 you believe and admit to terror, fear
 of failure, anger, rage, fury, blind hate,
 and the blood curdling infinite and unrelenting
 knowledge of betrayal and lies, double dealings,
 humiliations, and the ignominious self-sacrificing
 you are expected to offer up daily
 because in that bloody expulsion from the womb,
 at the moment you leapt into life,
 into the body of this world
 you came born as female.

STUDENT EVALUATION OF INTRO TO WOMEN'S STUDIES

(a found poem)

Intro to WS is a great place
to meet women.

I learned a lot.

I used to just look
at girls' breasts,
but women are really smarter
than I thought
since I've been talking to them.

The Test

1

My students bend intently
over their desks, the test questions swirling
around their heads, the answers gathering
or slipping away.

I have taken them to the wall
in *The Handmaid's Tale*
where Margaret Atwood hung the bleeding bodies.
I have taken them there and forced them to touch
the red-brown O's of mouths now silenced.

I have held in front of them the photos
of the Triangle Shirt Waist Factory girls
flying through the air, unnecessary angels.
I have held the photos before them
like a Veronica holding the sweated and bloody
face of the Christ printed on her scarf.

Touch these wings, I demand.
Touch the concrete before these women
smash against it like bags of groceries
you'd spill going into your house—
they are full of life, not bread and wine.

2

My students bend over their tests
intent on making the right responses.
It is required to test them this way
but I would rather send them
in the patrol car to the frat house

with directions to write up the rape.
Touch the semen up a co-ed's ass.
How many kinds of semen are there?
And let us count the ways it gets around.

Here, I say, here is a wound
to compare and contrast to no other.
Here is a little piece of culture
on a swab. Look under the microscope
and see this culture growing
like a scream in this dish.

This red mouth, this is culture's test
of manhood, of womanhood,
and this outrage I force into essay form
so you can write out
what we really know.

ASKING FOR AN INCOMPLETE

1

Please, she says, now I am sitting
in the courtroom to make my homework.

I can only make it in handwriting
while I am sitting in the courtroom

to see if my husband will take
my children. Please, I am not

a bad mother. I am not a bad student.
After ten p.m. at the shelter

they say, no more reading, no more
writing. Turn any writing

to the court. Maybe, they say,
I cannot finish this class.

Please, I am not a bad mother.
I must keep my children from him.

2

The holes where my eyes should be meet the holes
where her eyes should be (Greek statues, pre-classical period,
empty dark orbs where semiprecious stones once were set
by hand) and we are not at my eighth floor office door but grip-
ping each other's arms in the courtyard as the men swarm over
the wall 900 BCE, each with the face of my colleague
in ST 806 who has been looking disgustedly at the woman
crying, who watches my naked arm shielding her back,
my free hand smoothing her flying hair.

To Peter in Germany

1

Dear Peter,

I met three women this summer at Mono Lake. I knew they were foreigners because of their haircuts. I thought two of them might be dykes, and sure enough, they were East German lesbians. They had left their lovers at home while they were here doing research at the University of Oklahoma. I commented on what an out-of-the-way place they'd been sent to—like Oklahoma isn't exactly AMERICA—power center and all, but they thought they had seen the heartland. They were returning home to an uncertain future. What they said was their jobs weren't safe when men needed to be employed—that's what they believed. I could only sympathize and pet their dog. In Berlin the wall may have fallen, but it fell on the women. No female faces rose in the wave of grey suits on the tide of democratic revolution.

2

Homegrown atrocities
surround me when
I look at the women
who come to sign up for classes—
the tight smile of one

whose body
is a coin rubbed
between her boss' fingers,
the unlined, unlearned face
of a local beauty,
spent by 23.

Deferential,
they sit
in front of
my desk,
apologetic

as a season
out of season,
to say, "*it's just a feeling,
I've never read anything.*"

3

The dangers to my gender
are catalogued in the names
of foundations and social service agencies:
Haven House Shelter for Battered Women,
Alcoholism Center for Women, House
of Ruth, Sojourner, Lesbian Rights
Advocates, Beyond Survival.

The list goes on.

4

Dear Peter,

    *The effects you've seen of the Final Solution, built there
in a landscape and historical moment, I give you. I honor the truth
of the historical moment. When you come home to this city,
when you come back to your friends and your place in our his-
tory, I can only say I won't know who I am to you or to any man
anymore. I speak out of the dead mouths now, I speak out of my*

terror for the history of women as it comes before us in living
color and not as the dumb-show lie factory production which our
common culture drags out in moth-eaten costumes; and while
the tap dancing goes on, backstage is clitoridectomy, infibula-
tion, genocidal rape. The meter is running, Peter—more women
than Jews. Believe me, the sorry truth is more women than Jews.
More women than Jews, even. Hatred unto hatred. More. More.
More than we can count.

5

Dirty fingers.
It begins and ends
with dirty fingers. The priests can burn
all the incense in the world,
cut up all the sacrificial chickens
and throw blood on the walls, chant the laws
of eternity and not one thin
red running down white
trickle of it
matters to me.

In my lifetime,
even with forty years of feminism,
cutting the sexual parts out of girls
can still be practiced in the name of religion
and culture.

Want to answer the question of what 'eye for an eye'
I'm talking about here?
Want to know why the revolution is still an itch
in my palm, why I lose
whatever civilizing effects culture
used to have on me?

All the non-violence in the world
has not saved female bodies
from men
and their lies:
theology-lie, philosophy-lie,
regulation-lie, history-lie,

lie lie lie lie lie.

I grant no one the benefit of the doubt.
I speak their language now,
an eye for an eye, a part for a part.

I commit myself to kill
the pain
and what causes pain.
I commit myself
to the end of their world.

6

Dear Peter,

If a jawbone is found in the desert
separated from the body,
what's your guess, my friend?

Is it a woman?

Is it a habit?

Is it the natural law?

PASSING

LIVING HERE NOW

My father's dying
resembles nothing so much
as a small village
building itself
in the mind of a traveler
who reads about it
and thinks to go there.

The journey is imagined
in a way not even felt
as when years ago
I knew my father would die someday.

The idea came up as fast
as a curve in a road
which opens out
to an unexpected vista,

and now in this journey
the road gravel crunches
under my tires. I miss
some of the streets,
get lost, get lost.

I find I'm no tourist anymore
and settle into the oldest human assignment.
Bury your father and live forever
as a stranger in that town.

Los Angeles Is a Virgo

for Luis Alfaro

Born like me on September fourth, ruled by Mercury,
the eternal child is what the magazine horoscope promises,
though LA's a little older, a little dustier,
maybe even more varied than the crennalations
in my cerebral cortex,
more full of running glyphs
than the convoluted cranial bag of fits and starts
I've been juicing around in
since my own little 9/4 entrance
into the world of things and beings.

No wonder I love this city, song of myself.

Choose between little corner taquerias
and Thai home cooking joints, amazing
as the expectations of angel sightings
we daily live in, tongues of flames
leaping not from the heads of gods or laps of goddesses,
but from green and red and yellow chilies
swirling in the devil's brews along the boulevards,
little food stands in corner mini-malls
with four or six paint-stripped slots
to slip a car into,
then walk to the order-window,
pay and move quick-time
to the "take-out line / pick up food here station,"
the sliding glass door ringed with salsa cups,
straws in white paper sleeves, chili-flakes in a shaker
or "what do you call this?" condiment of the culture
from which this food is delivered and delivering us unto.

(oh, the tongue is so much wiser than the mind!)

Shrimp burritos, now where did they come from?
Fish tacos—it took me a long time to imagine them
without conjuring up an image of a mermaid in a blanket.
I would pass up a trip to Chinois if some local *vato loco*
could lead me to the right Cambodian market cum café
and point out the fish sauce that would light up my lips
like neon without putting me in a coma.

I am immoral in my desire to sniff the length of,
rub between my fingers, and roll around in my mouth
the flavors, bread things, and common seasonings
of all of my compatriots here
at the blue-bleeding westward sea-shelf of the Pacific
where the currents of human traffic move and cut
into each other like the vast mile-wide streams of water
streaking toward the poles, weaving into the web
of cloud, wind and weather systems that billow into space
like gossamer skirts, like a dancer's pantaloons.

And again the rivers of the earth, like a blue tattoo,
come into view through the cloud veil
which daily swings in and out
over Mother Sea, over Mother Hand-Me-Over,
Mother-Carry-Me-On.

Here's the common culture the anthros are looking for
when I try to order in my home-grown white girl Spanglish,
hoping that when they call my numero ocho y something
('cuz I'm bad at numbers in any language),
I'll pick up my own order and not some other
mother-tonguer's Polski Wyrob-strewn
seven-story-high Dagwood sandwich-to-go

with a Handy-Wipe and Pepto Bismol pink triangle
in the bottom of the bag (50% post-consumer waste,
soy ink, no fingerprints or bloody glove).

And off I'll go, swirling into the traffic, lunch in lap,
knowing I have three days to finish
all matters related to communication
since my ruling planet and that of my home town
is taking off backwards for three weeks
(the old Mercury-in-retrograde motion),
a little planetary hiccup
home town and I are both fabulously famous for.

LATIN FROM THE MASS

I

Yesterday we laughed
and said some Latin from the Mass,
the *Introibo* and the end.

Then I went off to work again
after we held the little plastic cup
to the light and lined the liquid up

and wrote the figures down,
your blood and something else
flowing from your side.

The video we watched about it,
"Cleaning Your Drains,"
called forth the wrong tone

for the feeling, the horror of remembering
a stranger with a spearlike scalpel
slicing off your breast,

leaving you nothing
but the base
of that small mound

threaded with black,
a little Gethsemani
or was it Golgatha?

Was it a crown of thorns
that slipped like an empty bandolier
across your breast?

We look through the opaque window
of the bandage to the scar
forming like a track over the wound

won in a war, or was it
just a raid?
Was it just a truce you made?

II

Tonight the little plastic cup
you held up

was full of fluid, pink
like cream in berry juice,

like a morning rose or dull carnation.
Tomorrow, if it goes well,

the yellow tint will clear
all the way up the tube

to where it leaves your side
and we will chart

the numbers at the line.
We will cry and laugh

and slap our thighs. No more mass
under your skin in mammogram,

but one breast paid the price—
that toss of dice

your cells played
on you.

I hold you while you shake
the lotion, spread it

on your newly forming skin
and touch the final line, and touch the final line.

THE BEACH AT SUNSET

for Colleen

The cliff above where we stand is crumbling
and up on the Palisades
the sidewalks buckle like a broken conveyer belt.

Art Deco palm trees sway their hula skirts
in perfect unison
against a backdrop of gorgeous blue,

and for you I would try it,
though I have always forbidden myself to write
poems about the beach at sunset.

All the clichés for it sputter
like the first generation of neon,
and what attracts me anyway

are these four species of gulls we've identified,
their bodies turned into the wind,
and not one of them aware of their silly beauty.

I'm the one awash in pastels
and hoping to salvage the day, finally turning away
from the last light on the western shore

and the steady whoosh of waves driving in,
drumming insistently like the undeniable data
of the cancer in your breast.

We walk back to the car
and take the top down for the ride home
through the early mist.

No matter what else is happening,
this is California. You'll have your cancer
at freeway speeds. I'll drive and park

and drive at park. The hospital
when I arrive to visit will be catching
the last rays of the sun, glinting

like an architectural miracle realized.
I realize a miracle is what you need—
a grain of sand, a perfect world

where you live beyond the facts
of what your body has given you
as the first taste of death.

POSTCARD

for Lynda Hull

> *"Today every-*
> *thing was glazed with ice*
> *after a brief thaw then a plunge*
> *in temp. So the news was*
> *full of spectacular 25 and*
> *40 car smash-ups.*
> *Weather & traffic as meta-*
> *phor? I won't touch*
> *that one!"*
>
> —postcard greeting from Lynda Hull

1

Found this message on a postcard from you
by accident about a month or so
after your death.

What did it matter then I'd stuck the card
as place marker in a collection of stories?
What did it matter then if you'd mailed it
from Amsterdam or New Jersey or Chicago?

Always in motion,
back and forth, faster and faster.
That was the danger—so much so soon.

One friend, seeing your picture in the paper,
mistook your obituary for an announcement
you'd won another poetry prize.

2

That line to me about weather and traffic
was just a joke—who supposedly knows less

about weather than a Southern Californian?
And who knows more about traffic
than a Los Angeles poet, anyway?

And who knew more about death
than you, the one who turned away
from that follow spot more than once,
the chanteuse who stopped shooting her blood
full of jazzy soporific juice?

Who knew more about flirting with death,
kiss-on-the-cheek flirting,
and smoky dancing thigh against thigh with it
down the chasm of love?

3

Everybody knew it would come, it would come
to end you earlier than most,
no old woman sitting in a room, dreary
on a white-sheeted bed.

It would come in high relief, it would come
like numbness in a needle, cold as overdose
even when you said you weren't using anymore.
It would come because it always comes—

just like Chet Baker falling out of that window,
just like falling in love with how blood is dark and tasty.

It would come because you were
a hand-leaving-glove kind of gal,
risky as rhinestones before 5:00 p.m.

4

Skinny saint, I would have put some meat on your bones
if you had slept with me.
But you were my guardian angel
and not anywhere near available for lust,
not anywhere near available to me
since I didn't need saving,
just revising.

My belated epitaph comes down to
this shambles of intention.
I have a postcard from you that set elegy in motion,
and it keeps tumbling like a mantra of remembrance
or a cajoling spell for more words,
more poems as deep and lush as trumpet bells,
poems to love for their sheen and tactile intelligence,
chiaroscuro in language your métier.

5

Come to your senses, I say. She is dead,
and I place that foreign feeling squarely in front of me
like the postcard of a room in which the chair of an artist
painted by another artist sits empty.

ASKING ABOUT YOU

Instead of having sex all the time I like to hold you and
not get into some involved discussion of what life means.
I want you to tell me something I don't know about you.
Something about the day before that photograph in which
you're standing on your head. I want to know about softball
and the team picture. Why are you so little next to the
others? Were you younger? Were you small as a girl? What
I want most is to have been a girl with you and played on
the opposite team so I could have liked you and competed
against you at the same time.

LOUGANIS

If Praxiteles had been an animator, this form
is the one he would have set in motion—
a spinning diver hurtling down
toward the surface of a pool,
its smooth skin raised to ripples
by an automatic wind machine.

He'd sculpt Louganis like a beautiful machine
poised against the cloudless sky, then charge his form
with action—the rippling
muscles of the torso tensing with explosive motion
as the diver vaults, kicks out and plunges into the pool
where cameras follow him down,

a sheath of bubbles wrapping him, down
where applause is a watery blur, the machine
of celebrity waiting above him, the press pool
of reporters eager to surround, touch his form—
a boy-god, perfect in stasis or motion,
an athlete who could ignite any crowd, send ripples

of excitement through an arena, ripples
of awe around the globe, even after he stepped down
from competition. I saw him once, pure motion
in a dog show ring, his Great Dane puppy not yet machined
into perfection. Greg was the one all form,
perfectly balanced on his toes, emerging from a pool

of dog handlers as the star. Outside a swimming pool,
nobody recognized him at first, but ripples
of applause picked up, formed
a little cup of sound, then settled down
again as he was one of us, no machine
of glory, just a guy and his dog in motion.

That was before rumors of HIV set chaos in motion
and sports shows ran films of his infected blood coloring the pool.
Predictably, the story fed into the tabloid machine,
and the customary scornful ripple
of reaction to anybody gay threatened to drive his name down
from Olympus, but no bigotry could change the form

of his achievement, no machine of hate or ripple
of fear for his life could alter the timeless motion into a pool
of a beautiful boy falling down from heaven into perfect form.

Torn Open

I

Martin Luther King a long time dead.
Watts and South Central still without malls
which mushroom everywhere else,
without supermarkets, but plenty of three mile trips
on public transportation to get groceries

What are we doing about it, anyway?

Just filming the fantastic array of sprawled limbs
in the nightscapes of drive-bys,
just covering the revival of Klan picnics
where white-hooded babies are held aloft,
just calling in talk-shows, disembodied voices
smoking through cellular phones.

II

I react like a white girl sometimes
and don't cop to my longing
to touch the darkest dark,
unloved for what of it is African.
I don't claim the full length
of a passing glance
between racial strangers,
but close my door shut
before I, too,
am seen.

III

More than a generation ago on TV
I saw the Mississippi sun shatter on the river.

I stared at the schoolboy faces
of Chaney, Schwerner and Goodman

in the newspapers
before their bodies were discovered,

dug up like roots
from a backwoods earthen dam.

I didn't take the physical
to go South with SNCC

and register voters or sit at lunch room counters
with black women and men.

I thought I would die on that freedom train,
the *good girl* would die

or I would speak undo-able things
for the rest of my days.

IV

It happened anyway
in another part of life's business.
Good girl died kissing a woman,
rose from her bed the next day
and went out into the altered landscape
shaken down, flooded by the river
of "Who I Am,"
what-to-keep panned out from *what-to-lose.*

That lover drew the big picture
on the wall. She had a color chart, too,
and my fingers followed the wheel
where she spun me, drew a dark line
around the body to throw it into stark relief.

V

In this city, only earthquakes bring out
the too simple humanity we crave.
Only what shakes us from our beds,

schisms one side of the street from the other
and takes a building to its knees
brings us to our senses and to each other.

Daily we live the unnatural disaster over race,
and the pulse of it
is spiked as a seismic printout
in the 8 point range.

The heart tries again to rally to the old songs
and the marching in the streets,
but years of neglect have been rumbling,
compressing into a spasm
which rends the ground of being open,
revealing its unforgiving maw.

Then we stand, mouths agape,
looking up and down our streets
for what is not yet fallen
to fall,
and what is not yet open
to break into flame.

SUITE FOR YOUNG MAN DYING

for Gil Cuadros (1962 – 1995)

1

Santa Ana winds cleaned the lanes
between the stars

and the night sky below the planetarium,
all the way down to Hollywood Boulevard, winked

like a strobe-ball
in a boy-dance bar room.

That was where I first met you,
where the streets opened out like fingers

and went searching,
went places you'd think they'd never go,

all of Silver Lake unfolding like a hand,
lifelines matching avenues and alleys,

and your own fingers venturing out
from yourself to trace the dusky incline

of a hollow cheek in shadow
or mark a place in a book where a phrase

honked like a curbside horn
and just took you away.

2

That was the whole scene then,
getting taken out of yourself by a look,

a whole book of them,
or the sweet smoky scents of leather jackets
blowing down the boulevard
Sunset east of Sanborn
from the bar named 3226
with its glade of neon palms
and hardwood trellis overhang.

Letting anything just take you away
seemed the only right thing to do.

But it was the beginning and the end,
the garden gate and exit from a leafy paradise
where kisses turned and fell
like poison letters from the end of the world.

3

Who knew the ways
AIDS would change everything?

I'm asking this
as if an answer will come ricocheting
off the graffitied walls
that read "silence equals death."

I asking this as if the pants and shirts
stitched into the Quilt
could put their gay boys on again
and go out dancing.

I'm asking this as if a chorus
of those sweet departed are waiting
to sing a healing song
and we could hear it if they did.

4

You lay there on your bed like a christos
down from the cross,
carved of wood stained dark
by extremes of exposure.
An Aztec sun rose on your arm,
princely in deep green-black ink,
and in ironic pairing,
your mother's embroidered tunic shone
with that same sun on her breast in yellow thread.
But not with the same heat or heart
did that sun beat.

5

The rest of you is petal pink

The rest of you is rust blue

The rest of you is a little locket

The rest of you is standing under trees

The rest of you is gas station guy

The rest of you is afternoon naps

The rest of you is a clay bowl

The rest of you is silly

The rest of you is stamps and envelopes

The rest of you is want not

6

I forget your early face.
Your final aspect
was somewhat on the way to grave,
but you nonetheless laughed
some lines into it
and appeared always alert
to a possible boyfriendly openness.

We traded poems back and forth.
We flailed at traditional forms together
and sunk some three pointers—sestinas
for both of us. We were tidy
and obsessed about our work.

You were handsome, I was handsome.
We were in a circle of poets for many years.
We were friendly about everything,
and admiring. You were a peach.

In your last days,
I admonished your mother and father
to take the world's opinion of you
as truth

for you were lovely, lovely.
You were just about everything lovely
except long-lived.

WHERE I COME FROM

for my mother

I come from having a job,
getting up in the dark
and dressing in the dark
and trudging downtown
before breakfast.

I come from being the breakfast maker
and the "good morning" sayer.
I come from owning the stools
where they hang their heels,
owning the ear they buy
with their coffee,
silent as the silent money
in the tray.

I come from going home after work
to bake pies, pie crusts and cakes.
I come from eating standing up
because I'm feeding others.
I come from in the alley, meeting
the man from Kitty Clover potato chips
and at the curb getting the donuts
from the truck, carrying the receipts
to the bank, checking off with a pencil
figures the teller reads back.

I come from being busy all the time,
the customer is always right,
our coffee is the best.

CHANGING WHAT WE MEAN

Turning your back, you button your blouse. That's new.
You redirect the conversation. A man
has entered it. Your therapist has given you
permission to discuss this with me, the word
you've been looking for in desire.
You can now say "heterosexual" with me. We mean

different things when we say it. I mean
the life I left behind forever. For you, it's a new
beginning, a stab at being normal again, a desire
to enter the world with a man
instead of a woman, and of course, there's the word
you won't claim for yourself anymore, you

who have children to think of, you
who have put me in line behind them and mean
to keep the order clear. It's really my word
against yours anymore in this new
language, in this battle over how a man
is about to enter this closed room of desire

we've gingerly exchanged keys to, and desire
isn't what's at issue anyway, you
say to me. Instead I learn a man
can protect you in a way a woman only means
to but never can, and my world is too new
when there's real life out there, word

after word for how normal looks, each word
cutting like scissors a profile of desire—
a man facing a woman, nothing particularly new
or interesting to me. I've wanted only to face you

and the world simultaneously, say what I mean
with my body, my choice to not be a man,
to be a woman with you, forget the man's
part or how his body is the word
for what touch can contain, what love means.
If this were only about desire,
you say, I'd still desire you.
But it isn't passion we're defining, new

consequences emerge when a man and desire
are part of the words we hurl, you
changing how you mean loving—this terrible final news.

From Los Angeles Looking South

Orderly traffic, a normal day
and 350,000 Salvadorians are in hiding
in Los Angeles.
Four women sit on the patio of El Rescate,
dirt packed hard from use.

Lydia's the weaver of this story
and two local women translate the Spanish,
pull the threads straight for me.

She has given this testimony for others
besides me. She's slight, simply dressed,
a former philosophy student, a suspect.

Her husband dead, her baby, living perhaps
with an aunt under another name.
Guernica again
hangs before us in the air
as the translators nod and check out
the current slang or a new word
from the war.

The sun is full strength
as I walk out onto Pico.
I take Lydia's testimony home,
stand out on my deck
and look south.

Down the hill, the banana trees
fan each other and two black dogs circle
in a fenced yard.
There are no people on the street
and cars pass like flashes of sun
through the pastel afternoon.

Not here, but somewhere else,
an incident in a field or at a gate
hatches the Guardia like flies.
The interrogation team changes tactics
to machine guns and disappearances.

Not somewhere else, but here,
the poem I am writing
already wonders about its worth.
I won't be shot for what issues
from the small house of my mouth
in this country of the tomb of language.

This poem will never need to lay a finger
to the lips of the person writing it
or head north
wrapped inside a bundle of my clothes.

Passing

These are the days that must happen
to you, Mr. Whitman says.

And the nights passing in succession
like images on film—

old movie star moon
filling up each frame then going into hiding.

People don't live long enough
to see the end

of their experiments.
At 24 frames a second it's soon over—

fireflies in the meadow,
games of children flickering in the park.

FROM
THE ISLANDS PROJECT:
POEMS FOR SAPPHO
2007

Audacious

How dare I speak
for Sappho?

How dare I say I
know the intention
in her line?

I say I know a door
when I see one.
I know cattle on a hill
and a cup of wine.

I know how an afternoon
is made and then tips
into evening.

I know a gesture carries
fire across time
and I know she
meant to speak to me.

How do you know what
Jesus meant except
feeling the words
pierce your heart,
align with your breath?

Hardscape

Say it's the memory of early mornings
in the shop, the power lift raising a car
in the dawn light, steam lifting off the highway
in front of the garage, and tools
coming to life at the touch of a hand.

Say it's the clang of things, the ping
of ball bearings pouring into a pan
and then a gush of gas from the pump,
the cleaning rag running over
the steely marbles to spark their shine.

Up the hill, the farm horse's shoes
tap against the gravel on the road,
the tack clinks and groans, the barn doors
bang and creak and corn stalks screech
against each other in the wind.

Say it made me hanker for hard things,
want to get outdoors first light, handle sticks
and dead tires, bang old mufflers together
and bam a ball peen hammer
against a scrap of sheet metal behind the shop.

It made me not want dolls and the demands
of indoors—quiet in the parlor, quiet by the stove.
It made me a woman of landscape and weather
and suspicious of my place. Say it gave me
a chrome handle to a different and difficult world.

The Grackle on the Lawn

She wants the blossom.
She wants the seeds in the grass.

She wants the beautiful thing.
She wants to eat.

It's so simple, she's like a person.

She wants the beautiful thing.
She wants to eat.

She's like a person, she wants to live
with that beautiful blossom and she wants to eat.

She flies off with the blossom in her beak.

WIND IN MYTILENE

and on the waves in turmoil
in the harbor
gulls floated
like pieces of paper
set adrift, little
boat-like birds
twirling
in the wind-tossed waves
that drove into
the strong arms of the seawall
at the apex of the bay
where a statue of Sappho stands,
young woman
with a lyre—not
looking out to sea
but glancing at the curve
of the seawall
and the birds,
those lost notes
before rain

The Living Fragments

for my mother

Her sentences broke verbs into bits,
her syntax shards of a time sequence
shattered in a swallow.
Some foreshock drug had pushed
a verbal precipice to slide
and dive to insane depths.

"When did I go crazy?" she would ask.
She wasn't crazy. She had many minds.
They all made sense, just like a word
on a fragment of papyrus means something
even when you know the rest are missing.

My mother would think I had children,
that she was cooking a roast, that dad was still alive,
so our conversation often ended up
like Scrabble in zero gravity.

It turned out we could talk about the Dodger game,
the Laker game, the spring flowers out the window.
Unbelievable that she and I were able
to piece together what she cared about at all.

So I read Sappho's fragments
with a trained eye. She is my other
blasted heritage, beautiful
in disarray, the aftermath
I didn't have happen
right in front of my eyes.

THE SINGING SCHOOL

I saw one narrow as a blade
in a man's black suit

I saw one drop her pages
on the floor and walk away
from the microphone like a bullfighter
turning his back on a bull

I saw one with generous breasts
in a floral print dress shift
from one foot to the other
while her body blushed all over

I saw one in pain, in pain
enough for ten strong women
but she didn't say a word about that
pain, she went deep under the water
and came back and she wasn't alone

I saw one who's breasts were cut off
and she sang anyway saying,
"Nobody cut my throat yet"

I saw one who mid-wifed the language
of her tribe and taught everyone
to dance to its music

I saw one comb through history
sifting the dust for rings, for broken links
of gold, for altar pieces and the altars, too,
for the shapes of animals and birds
in conversation and divinity in the tracks of deer

I saw one in her coffin strewn with roses
and lilies, the narrow heaven she made
rising around her perfumed and dense as diamonds

I saw them in their labor and I saw them laugh,
and all of them, all of them have passed down Sappho's street
in Eressos and stood at the beach
where the dark rock stands, where if you look carefully
you can see a lioness about to rise and go

TUTELAGE
for Sappho

I must admit I didn't think of you
when first I fucked a woman who had given
birth. Before, I'd learned with green and grassy
girls who clenched with furious delight my tongue
or thumb or fist. But this was a room in
another room, a world behind the walls
where men don't go, or if they do they fall
into the fear of capture. I fell, too,
but enraptured by the flesh of it all.
And taking me in, she took me too far
in my mind, she took me out its door, she
who only hours before had pulled my shoulders
through her car window, kissed me on the street.
Gripping me like life or death, she said
she wanted me to fuck her hard and harder
than I ever had and did I understand?
"Of course," I said. Of course, I lied or
only later knew the cost of truth.
Tutelage, means you'll learn. Tuition, you pay.

Why I Call on Artemis, Not Aphrodite

because there was no hearth
because there was no home
because there was no place or position

at the barricades
at the defense of the clinic
at the staging area

before the cameras arrived
before the demonstrations
before the broadcasts

in line for the signs
in rain and wind outside the building
in constant phone communication

where the buses embarked
where the flyers were printed
where the marchers gathered

doing the paperwork
doing the fact checking
doing the scheduling

because we were women
who met in the time of struggle
and loved in the alleys of ourselves

and fell to our knees in our knowledge
and fell on each other in thirst and hunger
and fell into love in an endless time of war

My Mothers

for Alicia Ostriker

My voice has three mothers,
my own mother, Carmen,
and Sappho,
both lost in history
for different reasons
but preserved in me.

I heard in my mother's voice
the inflections of her family,
my old Montana uncle
and the stones of the White Rocks
up where the Missouri River is born.

My mother in later life would fade a little
as evening came on,
her tone of voice shifting to Uncle Roy's
as if she had tuned into
a radio station on a long trip
across open country.

And Sappho I hear with my eyes closed,
the push of a woman
singing into my diaphragm,
thrilling as the hum of my mother's voice
when she sang to me as a child.

Whitman described it best—the "valved voice"
Where would I be without Walt?
Mother Whitman, as Alicia calls him.

Sometimes my Freshman English teacher
made light of him, the line "handkerchief
designedly dropped" and "my barbaric yawp."
I sat through the class, rehearsing poetry, knowing
in an inchoate way
what it would take
to sing in a woman's voice

as maybe Walt tried to do,
or maybe he just tried to sing
and a woman's voice joined him
from the soul of the world

The Day After Meeting Her

In the fourth year of my marriage
and in my parents' home
and in the little den
that had been my writing room
while I was in college,

I sat down and began
to make a history
of my sexual self

and there was always a woman there.

None of the words
was unfamiliar to me—
incense, apples, groves of trees—
or the catch in my breath
when a woman sang a song.

But the fragments reconfigured,
puzzle pieces moving
in three dimensional procession,
proof instead of excuse,

and in the fourth year
of marriage, my heart froze.

I was somebody else
to myself than the woman
who the day before
had gone to visit a friend
near the beach
and turned at the sound
of a voice
in the doorway.

A woman was standing there
in the way there had always been
a woman there—
incense, a catch in the breath,
the image of trees meaning love,
a list snapping into place,
fear that I might already know
what I was about to know.

This was in the fourth year of my marriage
and the year of my first book.
It was in the summer.
I went to the beach and back again.
I took off my clothes
and shook inside because

she was there
and there had always been a woman
in me

looking for her

Sappho, You Must Have Had a Mother

who died,
who slipped out of your life
and for awhile left you
with little to say,

and in that time,
did you have a daughter yet
who also cried and held onto
something your mother gave her?

I carried my grandmother's rosary
in the left front pocket of my jeans
for years. Just yesterday,
I took it out of the old jewelry case
grandfather gave me.

There was a bead missing
that I hadn't noticed before.
The wood of the cross was worn
and the silver of the cross was worn
so that the thin body of Jesus
looked like a shadow instead of a man.

When your mother died, did a ritual
move the grief through you
in the way it is said ritual does?

I don't have the kind of faith
I once had, so I find it's better
to think on the bead that is missing
and think of silver and wood
slipping through my fingers.

If There Were No Books

Where did you two girls
find time
and place
to be alone?

And if you couldn't bend
your heads over a book,
lean into and laugh
with each other,

how did you
touch
by accident,
and then because you wanted to?

Love Poem from Afar

for Colleen

I

This morning I'm more lonely than the sky,
that flattened tray of tin and rain

before the robin's quick array of ruddy breasts
displayed the air a way that's new

as when in their noisy gang
they flew against the blue

like stitches in a quilt
that's being aired out with a shake.

I take some solace watching starlings
with their yellow bills root among the leaves.

They're plump with some success, those clerks.
Field notes, perhaps, or a survey of the seeds.

II

Your day still sits under the horizon
while mine unfolds in steps I take
to make myself familiar here:
breakfast in the kitchen, carry tea upstairs,
watch a squirrel hop across the lawn,
keep a careful list of birds I've seen.
Tai chi, before or after.

I know we're on the same planet,
the same sun coming in the east window.
I know how and why time zones float
like gauzy curtains across the globe.
But here's the fact that sends me to the page.

I want to see you every day we're in this life,
mark change with you as we change, as we age,
for it's true, as you say, it took a long time
for us to find each other and much pain.

Being away, I think only of telling you
about these birds, these swales of rain
and flowering trees so different from our own.

This would be another world
with you in it.

No—you are the world

So the teacher jumped up on the desk
in our Freshman English class,
the front door to the mind for us little less than
middle-class Catholic girls at Immaculate Heart College, &
our eyes fixed on our professor, his spit flying,
his suit coat and tie flying,
him waving a little black & white copy of this *Howl*
like it's a hymnal and & he's got religion,
he's got the juju chant & rattle
of a million dead rosaries sent electrical
shock to revive & turn themselves into the
knuckle joints & knee bones of the living—
Let's dance it all started to say, let's
shake this thing, this hour, this book, this life
which is not going to be the one you registered
for—NO, you are not going to return to the
parish & iron the altar cloths. NO, you are not
going to carpool, learn golf, play bridge
on Tuesdays or join the Catholic Daughters
of America, you are NOT going to make
Jell-O molds & tat doilies, you are going
to smoke a lot of dope & waste the weekends
drinking gallons of Gallo Hearty Burgundy
shirtless on the patio & you won't be alone.
The Beatles are coming, the Beatles are coming &
you are getting a booster shot for anti-war proclivities,
you are getting so amped that language
will not rest like a four-cylinder low-mileage
car in your garage but turn into a nitro-burning
dragster in your guts—peeling, wheeling, weaving
from lane to lane before abandoning the pavement
altogether, airborne without a parachute.

You are ready for *flame out flame out*.
The sky opening like a mouth & wrapping its lips
around your paganized shoeless & blessed feet says
inhale the impetus to flee your former self,
ditch all your classes & go who knows where
or cares.

Working Towards Sappho

I

I can't always be sure I'm getting anywhere.
Maybe the clue is in the way Mytilene streets
drive toward the city center through
the stack and sprawl of squared off stones,
the one-way lanes and round-abouts.

I have to live in so many minds
to talk to Sappho about the books of law
that stand between us,
the Bible and the Koran,
books that rule a world
she knows nothing about.

And me, not knowing much of her,
not even knowing what "news"
meant in her life, what exile meant
and how she knew to leave the island
and if it was night or day when she fled.

Her approvals//the beautiful women.
But what fruit did she put on her table?

Invite Sappho and me into the same room
and what would we talk about?

She wouldn't know someone had walked
on the moon.
I wouldn't know whether she had a dog.

What did it mean to say what she said
in 600 BCE?

How did she feel about
her own beauty? Hints

she didn't make,
or they're missing.

The only through line
is the erotic charge around women

and that she loved her life

II

Would there be room in Lesvos
for Sappho now?

Little shrines along the roads
in the form of miniature churches
are stuffed with empty bottles
and cans of beer.

In the cafes, men talking, men loudly
talking to other men
in rooms that boom
with the voices of men
talking to men,
smoking and drinking.

Would there be room for her voice
in the overlay of sounds
of the men filling every vesicle?
From shrine to church to altar,
their images are pounded into icons

and the Infant Christ sits like a squalling ham
in the Virgin's lap.

III
*The Villa of the Papyri at Herculaneum, containing the
library of Lucius Calpurnius Piso Caesoninus, Julius Caesar's
father-in-law, was preserved by the eruption of Mount Vesuvius,
but has only been partially excavated.*

Another poet in another time
might live her lesbian life
with other facts
that come to light
in the unearthing of the library
at Herculaneum.

Down from antiquity, untouched
by the monks of the Middle Ages,
hundreds of carbonized scrolls burned and buried
by the eruption of Vesuvius,
now await their translators.

What could be found there?
Affirmation of Sappho's life as we know it,
or something entirely different?

Whatever emerges, a poem
written by a lesbian poet
has a heritage of flame,
and no matter what Sappho was,
any woman who "comes out"
springs from a burned life
as a poem.

IV

I can't know if Sappho
would understand
all the facets of my life.
I've lived with one woman
for almost twenty years.
We're not alone in this.

But I believe Sappho would understand
the moment when one woman
has been circling the other
for an hour or so,
a look in her manner
tense and vulnerable.

Sappho would put down
whatever instrument
was in her hands
and go to her.

This is the moment and the bond that begs
affirmation.

This is the rest of the story
writing itself among us.
The future must bristle with the names of women
like fragrant cloves in an orange,
like quills on a healthy porcupine,
like hexagonal columns of basalt
that rise from the earth
and cool in the shape of cathedral naves

It can be known, it has been written, it can't be changed.

Not Disappearing

The poems I write
to you, Sappho,
seem bird-bone light
in comparison
to my poems about cars
and the freeway
and the heavy-metal centuries
in which I've lived.

Something disappears
when I talk to you,
and it also happens
that each word's history
leads to a question—

what nouns and verbs
could we share
straight up?

I think the most beautiful words
are drifting, smoky things
with such long histories
you would have known them
as I would know them:

dawn,
the moon,
waves and boats,
laurel trees.

I think we both know the meaning
of a line of women walking
back from the beach,

some singing, some
carrying baskets—
and one who runs ahead,
runs not in a direct line,
but dips like a swallow—

and a cloudless pale blue sky.

When Did a Self Begin?

In memory of my mother, Carmen V. Klein, 1922 – 2006

I

Eared wheat, silky corn, squash blossoms
at the bulbous end of a squash, that vegetable umbilical
squirreling through the garden, around the gate post,
its tendrils like ringlets of a green god rising and twining.

This is what I know from childhood,
pictures in my mind for growth.
I could add the animals straying in their pastures
or stolid in pens in the farmyard,
or the daily industry of egg laying in the chicken house
and the chickens pecking in the dirt.

Where did a self begin then?
Not to speak of me, but her.
Hair cut straight across her forehead
in photographs, hungry eyes.
Even now they say hunger, but not as deep and dark.

II

Childhood in rural South Dakota.
Rough row to hoe, everybody says it.
If you didn't grind and till and plow,
and even if you did and the rain didn't come
or spring frost killed the shoots,
if the food didn't come up
out of the ground,
you starved.

But her great-grandfather kept the eggs
to give to the plow horses for their coats.
What economy of scale explains this?
Her own mother, sickly all her life
and dead at age fifty of leukemia,
most often a childhood disease.

Where did my mother begin, then?
In scarcity, in the dry rows at the edge
of the cornfield where the watermelons
lay heartless after pillage. The boys from town
or the tramps on their way to the river taking the best.

Each younger sister taking something away.
Time spent untangling the curls of the sister
who cheated and the sister who lied.
Cooking the one steak for the sick mother
who grew up on bacon grease sandwiches
carried to school in the small black tin.

My mother's father at the tractor yelling
as she began to turn over the engine,
"be the boy in the family."

She the one yelled at most,
made of other people's demands.
Nightly fearing the sleepwalking sister
would tumble down the stairs
and she be blamed,
though more often than not
the sister was found in the morning
covered with quilts in the bathtub.

III

Measured against the river undercutting the bank,
what force would be the one to point to?
The swelling tide of a small family
or war and disease and three children
to raise during hard times?

What river cut the bank out,
left no island, instead a tearing away of soil,
the sound of deep roots separating
from the flat planet of prairie and sailing away?

I learned to fear standing too close to the river
out there in the pasture, the car left running
while the grownups walked to the edge
to watch the flood carving a new river bed,
knowing the wet hollows would spring
with mushrooms, that hundreds of pale heads
would rise from the mysterious spoon-like depressions
where rocks had rolled away
in the current and downstream.

They were the other children of the floodtide,
drowned and drowned again forever.

That swamped and silent life
leaving its impressions, its shadows like thumbprints.
Identity flowing onward, then gone by, forever gone by.

IV

There were vast monochromes she could stare into,
horizontal beiges stacking like lines of muted music
if she could but reach to hear it over the constant wind.
The striated sky lowering until the horizon disappeared
and the tornado clouds came up, the birds silent,
animals huddling in the corner of the field,
the lowest place where the creek shoveled under
the barbed wire fence, the grey posts
with their roots hanging free of their tether to earth.

Then more wind, blocks of blue-black chunks
like slate stacking and twirling,
like the way she starts to think—a habit of mind
that's a confusion of ends and means—
sky gone dark to storm and swirl,
stunned there like the plains tipping on their axis into night.
Then little stars stabbing through, stuttering for hours
across the great black flatness after wind.

Her aunt, once picked up in a tornado and flown a mile,
had cornstalks driven through her ears.
She could hear only through the soles of her feet.
Cars and trains sang up her calves. She would sway
side to side, reach a hand out to someone,
a problem with balance besides the silence.
That story was told me by my mother
when as a child I met my great aunt
and we all posed for a photo—four generations,
north, east, south, and west—
and me down there in the corner
close to the paper anchor that held the picture
fast to the page.

V

The summer sweltering, main street a stew
of wavy heat steaming up from the pavement
and the road tar melting mid-day.
She sways in the restaurant kitchen and stumbles
to the counter where a man catches her.
Someone runs to get dad at the Ford garage.

I am nowhere to be found, down by the creek
with Tiny and Big Boy and Carol, digging crayfish
out of the mud. It isn't hot down in the culvert.
We only know how hot it is
when I get home and she is down
on the bed with an ice bag on her head.

Heat stroke, that's what they say.
She comes to, looking like she took a punch,
but rises at the bell next morning for work,
dips a handkerchief in ice water
and ties it around her neck.
Calcium deficiency, the doctor declared.

What did the heat heap on her then?
A knock-out, dad says, just like when Rocky Marciano,
pale as a chef's uniform, knocked out the champ,
Joe Louis. Hard to fathom for a seven-year-old
that your mother could fall over in the middle of the day.

VI

Under the anesthetic, she dies
into the hands of another and returns,
the gases in her blood crossing
back to the proportion and balance
of the living. I sit like a scribe
in the outer chamber waiting room
while her soul comes back
into the wrapper. Keeping track
is my ordinary task, doing some work
while I worry how she will make her way back
into the stitched and bolted frame of her body.

She was somebody more and less new
after each of her fourteen surgeries.
She begins again in a different pose.
One time she cannot turn her head
more than 40 degrees off-center,
one time she cannot lower her chin
enough to see her feet and forever after
she returns to a clever trap, her body,
which she must elude in sleep or dreams.
The question is, did she ever fully come back
into the moving world again?

VII

Into a ceramic grid of snow-white tile,
she falls face first onto the bathroom floor
in the retirement home.
She falls toward a blankness she lives in
for some months, her face maroon
from forehead down to her mouth,
a waterfall of blood inside the skin

She doesn't remember it.

Nor does she remember a white rush of opiates
whiplashing out of her body
from the wrong dose of morphine.
Nor the five paramedics who carried her
out of the house and into the ambulance,
her yelling, "He's not dead,
he'll come for me. He's somewhere
just down the street, my husband, Ray."

When I first saw her in the emergency room,
she was a gauze-trussed mummy,
shaking as if she had been plugged
into the 12 volt outlet on the way to the hospital.

VIII

"Your mother has died."

That's the phone call I'm always waiting for,
but it could be the boy crying wolf.
The good shepherd, the bad boy, the bad shepherd,
the good boy, the beneficent wolf.

Then, I'm in Ohio and the standby doctor
from intensive care calls about her DNR.

"The language is confusing," he says, "what does she want?"
I have a voice for this, the good daughter on top of things.
We have talked it over and over. She has bought her plot
and she told me casket closed. I'm ok with it all, I'm ok,
but ever waiting for the next call, the one for "next of kin."

I'm ready for this. Herself without me in the rain
of grief I'm in. Herself, can she begin again?
Can she find the door to a next life
swinging open, can she settle into
a better body next time?

I wish her one that has a full and happy laugh,
the one I heard when I was twelve, when on my birthday
she and my aunt got drunk and sang "Sweet Georgia Brown"
but never did that kind of crazy thing again.

IX

Crazy, a word with angles in it and letters
that can get you far away. Cracking noises
and a sharp buzz. I look in her mouth and see
her bottom teeth and her jaw set. She's gone
into another spin and now it sets in,
reminding me of my aunt, that day she came into our yard,
her hair a Brillo halo crackling with blue sparks,
her eyes whirling into space and back again.
She was drunk or crazy,
and those were pretty much the choices.

It terrified me to see my mother's face
could get that look, angry and white,
spraying spit and foam,
her voice a corridor of gravel and ice,
"Come here, come here, come here."

Daily life is a wheel and all it ever means
has rolled on past. Hallucinations replace it.
The dead come in and out of my mother's room.
Chickens crowd the Post Office. Don't I see them?
What's wrong with me then? She screams
to make sure someone hears her—"what's wrong with me?"

X

May 2004 and all the nurses and doctors on 2 East
have known this woman a month.

Six months ago she was my mother.
They didn't know her then,

the one busy in the crafts room
painting ceramic Christmas trees by the dozen.

Nobody had made the terrible mistakes with her meds.

They think she's the woman in 250 C who screams
"help me right now," who falls out of the bed each night

and, well, forget it, I tell myself. Tenth life for this cat,
and god bless her and who she will be next.

XI

3:20 in the morning.

I know on the first ring she's gone,
snuck out in the middle of the night
and died without me there.

When we arrive at the hospital
my mother is lying quiet as a mouse.
I stroke her brow, and kiss her hands and cry
and put my head on the rails of the bed.

This is the old body I know so well,
and the day, and the day, and the day
that was coming.

Two weeks ago she stopped
eating and drinking and speaking.
The nurses say it's common, the person decides.

XII

Last week on the "Days Gone By" page
of my home town paper, *The Remsen Bell-Enterprise*,
a snapshot from 1948.
My grandparents are off to Luxembourg.
At the train depot, family and friends pose.
I have no memory of this event,
but when I see the photo I cry anyway.

My mother, the living one,
stands in the front row.
She's holding somebody's baby in one arm
and has me by the hand.
My hair is blond and I'm wearing long pants
under my winter coat.

Oh, I know this muse-child
standing so close to her mother,
the dreamy smile and expectant look.
I will always be her only child,
though I don't have a clue yet what it will mean.
Later I realize it's a life's work, that love.

That mother, this child.

A WILD SURMISE

A WILD SURMISE

for Colleen

Like a bride of old,
I left my house and home

to come to you, to live
in that country that had no name.

All that I was, all that I had
came to you with a wild surmise

that some other world
was trembling

and opening. There were stories
to be written and told.

What colors would fill
those skies? What songs

of birds? There was never
a hint of Paradise or its alarms.

We knew that we would be
the wilderness and all that can be found there.

More than twenty years on, we are the trees
and we are the two rivers—

one brown, one blue—
and the ocean they become

after furious travels and falls,
rapids and deep pools.

We have seen as much
in ourselves and in one another,

living parallel yet knit together
feather upon feather.

No one else, no one else can claim us,
only the expansive and beautiful world

always before us
like that peak in the Darien,

always inside us, about to blossom
with the proof we are her own.

Fragments of a Grecian Urn

Striking and original use
of perspective on this fragment—

the foreleg of a white cow,
and a garland of some sort.

A bush with large blossoms
fills the left side of this triangular chip.

Another large fragment features the wheel
of a cart or carriage (abduction marriage?).

It's a celebratory event, certainly,
with so many sandaled feet in a procession.

These two pieces, if joined, reveal
hands clasping, but it's hard to determine

whether male or female,
there being no garments visible and the skin tone is so similar.

Here's such a small fragment,
that even under a microscope

the incised lines are barely evident
and the shade of red

is the color of a drop
of blood in water.

Faint text on this one reads "is truth . . ."
and "beauty [   ] all"

BIG DOG PHOTO

In memory of Primo (Fairhaven, Isle of Skye 1995 – 2007)

I

Your black wavy coat shone
like the sun inside out.
You always smelled like sun, too.
Black sun, clean-black as the afterimage of a falling leaf.

II

I apologize for what I said
in the poem "Dogs Out of The Kitchen."
The kitchen is a mess without you. I am so sorry
not to have recognized one of your charitable works.
You were a canine Teresa of Avila,
Saint of the Clean Floor, but with a better temperament.

III

I'm waiting for you to romp into my sleep,
that dream strewn meadow
where the wildflowers are just a memory now.

There was a path where I walked uphill
with Pauline through the Indian Paintbrush.
There was a stream where Zabi pinpointed

her steps along the verge.
You didn't know those places, urban
and urbane as you were.

The afterlife has its attractions.
If you are there now, I'm willing to adopt
a new belief system.

I would trade some of my years
if you could use them
and be in this life again.

My arms rehearse your shape, brush along
the angle of your ears, circle your deep chest.
This is what the catechism warned about,

attachment to things other than god.
Love of another body
without distinction and with pure delight.

Calling Upon the Saints Including Titanium

So, here is my little altar and some prayers.
I have a metal of the day and a bird of the day.
For this occasion, titanium—light and easy
to carry—and Peggy the Scrub Jay
for a satisfying flash of blue.

For the wisdom of the left hand
the prayer of the defeated,
and for the wisdom of the right hand
the song of the innocent friend.

For the forehead, a moment of solace,
mint-based and fragrant,
and for the chest where the heart lives,
a clean wave from the sea
to lift and float the body.

For the feet, ponds and streams,
and for the eyes, vistas in the style
of Wáng Wéi and also the poems
that go with them.

River stones and pearl gravel
for relief of the mind,
and a river bending in the distance,
a soft blue curve under clouds
with earth tones waiting.

I have roads, too, that weave
between mountain passes.
They are stories with such positive endings
I have saved one for the day I die:
Highway #395 north of Olancha, California,
where the Sierra Nevada shapes the vista
to the north.

At the Altar of the Peregrine

Chan Chich Lodge, Belize

This is how
you will go to god,

headless
upon his clotted breast.

You will lose your light
to a sudden brightness,

the stele of your speech
struck smooth

by the sweep
of his wing.

He will taste you
by daylight.

He will call
through your bones

like the compass-heart
that brought you here

to the altar
of the Peregrine,

this blue plateau
laced with Kingfishers,

those liquid jade prayers
flowing in the forests' veins.

Persephone and Demeter

In another version of the story
the daughter loses her mother.

Like a landscape at dusk,
like winter and the frozen field

the mother's body
has slowed to a stop.

What color of sheet covered her
in the emergency room

the daughter will not remember.
It is all snow flurries

and the bright berries
of her mother's blood

have lost their turning spin.
The daughter cannot raise this earth

from its stillness, cannot stroke
the blood back into motion.

From one hell to another
the daughter now clambers,

season after season
writing the story of snow.

MR. TWISTER

Mr. Twister and his sister, dicey doggy dots flee around the tree. Bumpy, rooty-tooty, slappy wavy footy left, footy right. Doggie dervish dashing out of sight. In a hurry, furry flurry, tasty tangy, the air goes blurry. Better do this, oh! I worry. Scratch a patch, leash and dash. Here we go. It's a blast of dare air, comb the hair wear. Talk about a walk!!

Commissioned by Susan Silton and included in The Tornado Project

Memorize This

The Green Honeycreeper
The soft jade chrysalis of Blue Morpho
The green anole lizard
The broad green leaves of the cecropia
The green adventurine stones in a bracelet
The green of green of green
in dracena, agapanthus,
heliconia, water lily,
beetle back, iguana, Palm Tanager,
Green-backed Heron, Coppery-headed Emerald,
Resplendent Quetzal, Turquoise-browed Motmot, Amazon Kingfisher,
the green of swirly Sarapiqui River swimming in its banks.
The green rind lining the sunset,
the green fall of night, the deep green sleep
in the jungle's lap.
The restless green dream
clearing its throat, shuffling
the celadon pages of its story,
the neon green letters saying "the end"

The Summer She Died

Rest in peace. That just about says
Everything—for her, but not for me. My shaky hands hold
The photo, her face less than the size of my thumb.
Unless I'm mistaken, she seems
Relaxed, standing out in the back yard
Next to the orange tree the summer she died.

Perhaps this is how memory works now.
Longing that never, never
Ends and always finds
Another missing piece. Like her
Smile, not in this picture, but
Ever on her face.

*Based on a photograph with the words "Please return" handwritten on
the bottom of the photo.*

Written for Other People's Memories/Found Photos: A Dialogue
With The Anonymous, *an exhibit curated by Paula Gray*
Mendocino College Art Gallery
September 13 – October 11, 2007

OH, DR. SURGEON

cuidado

because what if my wrist locks in place like a rusty gate and whatever I have
in mind can't get through, whatever I try to hold can't catch. What if the
hinge there is too old to repair and forever after all my shirts will not tuck
right, drying off with a towel will hurt me hurt me, drying my hair will
hurt and pulling up the covers hurt and worse, everything I go to touch
will have to be thought through, thought through even when there is a
vocabulary of impulse

right there is in the air at the end of my fingers, stories spun by the little
bones in their tiny dance. It is not enough to speak, you know. It is not
enough to have the words to say things. There is that moment, you know,
when something has to hang in the air. Hang in the air for a moment, and
turn

not on the tip of the tongue, the pointed slippery tongue, but here en *el
diccionario de mis dedos, las palabras huesudos* clicking cumulative as a litany,
running repetitive and desperate to find a saint still awake to gesture,
someone who in the past has worked miracles with the touch of her hand
and can still identify with the little needs of the living, a saint of small
things like The Little Flower, who understands dusting and folding, who
probably hurt herself and dipped her hand in Holy Water or cried out just a
little and then only in private

if I could pray anymore I would return to the rosary because it is filled with
wood and jewels, because I carried my grandmother's in my pocket like a
talisman for years, because even with a simple string you can make one if
both of your hands work, because when I can't sleep I can repeat the prayers
attached to suffering, to joy, to memory, to the blessedness of what comes
around again, familiar and whole.

Looking Up at the Ceiling

1

Two days there's been a door ajar
in my immune system
and hints of an intruder.

My holistic physician prescribed
salt water, zinc tablets, Vitamin C
and Yerba Santa capsules.
My solution—go to the movies.

2

Now I'm in my bathroom, staring overhead
while gargling warm salt water.
The ceiling's the texture of the moon's front side,
a silvery screen bouncing back
the glow from the light bar above the mirror.

Freshly painted walls already show
a new crack where corner meets corner.
I've seen its twin zigzagging through
the white tile around the bathtub
from an unnamed earthquake fault whose jolt
has made its presence known
as this lightning bolt.

3

You can guess where this thought is going, can't you?
It's shifting a mile off underground.

My death is building itself out of incidents
starting with my birth, my various broken bones
and system failures of one kind or another,
the little slippages that barely register in a life.
Richter-wise, they're nothing more
than a bad edit in a movie
or dropped syllable in a voice-over.

In the mirror, there's someone working her way
back to sucking her gums like a baby,
twisting the hair on her head in little circles with her fingers,
a shiny drop of something like the ocean
running down her chin.

The Arborist

She was obviously a Mourning Dove tipping
her tail down before landing in the upper limbs
and the spring-sprung leafing out that marks
with crayon green the empty spaces
gardeners opened late last fall when
for the first time in twenty years
that tree was trimmed.

I didn't have to look to know how she came
to land. She made the sound that Mourners
make, a swirl of silvery whistles
as she flew into the tree top

whose stub-ended branches spread wide
in a half-circle. They were shaped by the trimmers
to likewise fill out fan-like so the crown's profusion
of leaves would bloom into a perfect bouquet.

I didn't need to look to know the cut limbs
weren't pointed like the fingers on a hand. This
I learned by painting trees in the style
of Chinese brush paintings. At first, I drew
the ends of the branches out into fine tips,
but my teacher—and then the trees I started
to observe with skill—showed me that branches
bulb out at the end, thicken
where the growth comes from.

But when I turned at the sound of wings again,
the bird disappearing from the boughs,
only the joy of it was such a surprise.

AFTER SEEING THE HOCKNEY RETROSPECTIVE

in memory of Frank O'Hara

So what about my job?
>Summer is coming and the rainbirds
>>will sing sweet songs in the late afternoon.

And somebody, probably in the Valley,
>will have a pool party
>>where you can swim naked

because most of the women
>will be like Hockney,
>>pretty colorful and into the homoerotic.

Oh, bless our toasters and our trees,
>bless all the curvy roads
>>and spicy stucco.

Let's take down the wintered garlands
>of other people's gardens
>>and let the sprinklers flow again.

Hockney is painting in beautiful Los Angeles.
>Already water is filling the pipes,
>>already summer shirts anticipate us.

It Didn't Seem Dangerous

for that sweet dog, Pauline

It didn't seem dangerous in the dream
that my dog Pauline was riding
on the back of the motorcycle
or that I was driving
like a bat out of hell.

Gravel, there was a lot of
that, but no blood.
There was mud, though, and leaves
flying up from a track
through a forest.

Not a dangerous forest
but one that served
as a pale scrim
against which we drove
our dark night narrative together.

Even as I kept my eyes on the road,
I could see Pauline behind me, leaning
into the turns, and I was amazed
she hadn't fastened her paws
around my waist to hang on.

When we flew off the cliff
and were falling toward the churning rapids,
it finally felt dangerous
until we hit the water.
Mainly, I was worried
about Pauline, but she lit
onto a current and bobbed
away in front of me, careful
to turn and give a wave.

She was nothing but heroic
in my dreams, dangerous
as they might have seemed
if we'd suffered them
in the daytime.

I must admit in real life
she was pretty well-balanced
about what I put her through, me suddenly
a dangerous young woman
who had forgotten her normal life,
burning up brake pads driving us home
at night on canyon roads

while under my neglected sink,
little red potatoes sprouted
hordes of baby thin-shelled roaches,
eager for their albino chance to rule the dark.

REDEEMED

And we shall all be in our good bodies, washed in the blood
of the Lamb. And Christ shall come from a golden cloud
and sit at the right hand of the Father. And the Father shall
call out our names and in an instant all our sins shall
be known to the multitudes. And we shall all be
known to each other in our wickedness.

It was in the fourth grade at St. Mary's School
when Sister Perpetua told us what our fate
was to be at The Last Judgment.

We would stand in the largest crowd
we had ever known,
in the healthiest body we had ever worn,
and God the Father
would tell everyone our sins.

I've always wondered what would happen
then when everyone who'd ever lived learned
I had stolen matches from the church
and taken home a marble from school
which I did not return.

Not that any facts got in the way
of my fear of that reckoning.
For example, where would everybody stand
and how could anybody hear
over the tumult such a crowd would generate,
even if nobody but God the Father was talking?

And some of us would be two years old
and some would be in our teens,
and how would anybody actually be in a body
older than 40 years of age?

I should add it had always concerned me
that the mental age of each person
was not factored in—thus, some sins
would be more embarrassing
to those who heard about them
than to those who committed them,
and where would the justice be in that?

But since I have been redeemed,
I don't worry about the Last Judgment any more
than I do about the last payment on my house.
Forgiveness, it turns out, is capacious
when all we had been taught
was that it was capricious.

I was redeemed when I turned
and went back to Sodom,
to the friends and neighbors
I had lived among all my life.
Nothing untoward happened except
I didn't count myself among the fearful anymore.

I don't remember if my redemption
took place on a Sunday or not.
Stores were open, the markets
were full of shoppers buying food.
We greeted each other
as we passed in the aisles.

It was as if nothing had ever set us apart
in our lives. We didn't even fear death
because it was just another experience
we would share at some time,
either near or far in the future,
but certainly beyond our current sense of things.

THE WARRING STATES PERIOD

I

Studying the list of Chinese dynasties,
I soon come to The Warring States Period,
two hundred and thirty-one years from 480 – 249 BCE,
paralleling the time the area of the Parthenon
was just a sheepfold,
about 150 years after Sappho was born.

II

My birthday places me in the middle of WWII.
I was born in wartime and lived most of my life
during hot and cold wars.
They were never really as far away
or "foreign" as we used to call them.
Even now there are chapters
of the Veterans of Foreign Wars,
the battles of their wars living inside them
and not one soldier ever able
to return to a spring or autumn period
before the warring state became his lot.

III

Viet Nam was my war
because it changed everything I thought
about my country, my 'tis of thee.'
Every night the body counts broadcast
across the dinner table on the nightly news,
Nixon's secret Cambodia invasion leaked, and weeks later
Kent State students gunned down
while I was teaching a high school class.

After that war, I gave up on the truth press secretaries tell
as I had given up on Charlie McCarthy
once I was old enough to not look at the dummy
but at the man whose lap he was sitting on.

IV

Folded in a wooden glass-topped case in my workroom,
the flag under which my father's coffin rested
in the dim light of Lady's Chapel.
The crowd that came to his funeral mass
spilled onto the street.
Young guys and the retired,
best boys, able gaffers,
special effects men
and some of my father's buddies
from 885th Ordnance/China Burma India (1943 – 1945)

Men of work or war, my father both.

V

On my bookcase, I keep a small jewelry box
dad made for my mother
from a cast-off mortar shell.
It opens with a pleasant ring,
much like the chime of the Tibetan prayer bowl
sitting on the poetry shelf that starts with
The Art of the Lathe by B.H. Fairchild
and ends with *Clean Energy Verse*,
a chapbook of poetry from 1979,
"The Plutonium Ode" by Allen Ginsberg
autographed by him, page 12.

VI

All warriors, all flags. all lie down

SELLING MY MOTHER'S HOUSE

Here is the treasure map,
erasure as measure,

and what was she thinking
while pinning these pins,

and whose vest was this
and what did it match?

Where are the Wheat Back pennies
in the rainbow of dust,

the Lady Liberty silver dollars
that must never be spent,

and coins of the realm of silence
and coins of the realm of tears?

Where is the stamp block, the first day cover,
the collectible from Certified Dreamtime?

Let me shake the tin plate
passed down from Grandmother,

let me push the button
on the back door knob,

right twist the Dial-A-Lock on the workshop
and drop the steel rod in the sliding door track.

I seem to have missed everything—
the alarming X's on the calendar, the sibilant drapes.

There was one kind of money
hidden in the bread drawer

and another kind of money
in the embroidery thread box

and money that should be
somewhere but isn't.

The only treasure left,
the empty living room where my father died.

THE LAST BREAKUP

Maybe if she hadn't dyed her hair purple
and if she had gone to class
when I dropped her off each day,
then maybe she wouldn't have
gotten a heroin habit
and completely crashed your car.
If she hadn't gone to jail and
if you hadn't had to call your ex-husband
to meet you at the lock-up,

and if I had been the one
in family therapy with you
at the hospital instead of him
those three months of weekly sessions,
then maybe you would have
seen her talk to me
the way she talked in the car
on the way to school,
her hair glossy as a grackle,
back-combed on the top, nape
shaved, a perfectly crafted
punked-out geisha teen.

If you had seen her talk to me
then you would have known
I was her family, and not
like the one your mother had in mind
when she said "you need a man
to take care of you."
If you didn't take that advice so
to heart, then you could have
heard your daughter talk to me
about me moving in with you,

and if she hadn't painted
her bedroom black and ruined
the apartment so that your lease
was broken and you had to move,
maybe you wouldn't have said
she had to live with her dad
and his so-called bitch
who smoked dope all day.

If she didn't find heroin
then maybe she wouldn't have
felt superior to that stoner step-mom
and had to run away again
because there was no home with you
to go to.

If she had had a home
maybe she wouldn't have
needed a motorcycle
to make you mad at her some more
and you find my defense of her
tedious, and if I would have been a man
I would have told you to "calm down"
and you would have believed me.
Instead you said you had to
find a man and be normal again
and you wanted me to make that all right,

but by then I was so
bereft, as if my chest
had been unbuttoned in a
blizzard, I couldn't say
that it was fine for you to leave me,

to believe that admonition of that mother of yours
whose boyfriend was "hit" by the mob.

If you had just let me attend
family counseling and if you had
heard your daughter talk to me,
I think we had a home to make.
I did.

SINCE YOU ASKED

for Laurien Alexandre

Since you asked if I'm writing about current conditions,
I would have to answer that I'm not.
What's left to say more than Rukeyser already did?
The second century of the wars has rolled out and I have to wonder
if lies can get any more lie-like.

Current conditions and high tides altogether too predictable.

The nectarine in the paper bag on my counter—
now *that* demands a decent use of nouns.
Adjectives, yes, I drench the mangos with them.
Even ripeness needs some help. Words
that have the taste of truth.

I listen to the crows' morning complaints
and set out peanuts for the scrub jays.
I bury a little brown twig in the gravel
with the toe of my shoe.

This I can manage.

But since you asked, I'm writing with a brush
in place of a pen, smelling the sweetness of the ink stick.
I'm painting tree limbs and bamboo leaves,
sometimes waking from a dream of jade and amethyst,
mulberry paper and silk, able to go on again.

I try to live in a noble way, think of the good meanings
of ritual objects and the tastes of spices and fruits.
In the back of my mind, I hold at bay the feeling of
powerlessness, the feeling of betrayal, each day
asking of the current true believers who want to run the world,

"What do you think we are? Stupid?"

SHRINE AND ASHES

in memory of Zabi (Hunter-Pisces Zabione, 1991 – 2004)

Today it's your collar and tags
I buckle around the blue velvet bag.

Yesterday, the sentimental saying embroidered there
I turned to face the wall.

And the day before that, at the vet,
we picked up the cardboard box with your ashes in a vase

delivered from the pet cemetery crematorium
in the far end of the valley to the west.

The day before that, I lit a candle
I found in the drawer

and put it in the silver candlestick
with a tiny thumb-hold for a handle.

And before that, I put the picture frame
with photo of the puppy pen

we built for you, the snapshot a little out of focus,
but you were sharp, front and center, with toy.

And the day before that, no good news.
You'd gone downhill faster than we thought,

a sharp drop-off from our high hopes
that maybe you could come home from the hospital

and we could keep on carrying you
up and down the stairs.

Denial is as steep as that, old pet.
And the day before, and yet.

Wáng Wéi Did Not Paint a Fire

Wáng Wéi, 701 – 761, Tang Dynasty
Poet/Painter, Southern School of Painting

What is missing is anything
that Wáng Wéi painted,

so no one else could paint a copy of his painting
of a fire.

But, he wouldn't even have painted a fire.
Look at the "idea copies" of his hills.

There's nothing in his work like the tufted hides of brush
that cover the canyons here.

A fire has many colors of black and white
that Wáng Wéi never had to think about.

In autumn, the sky is full of them, slips of ash
and embers flying,

the heat signature of trees
writing their yearly saga

in smoke that drifts low
and then out to sea.

A wash of grey at the undulating horizon—
with a clean brush,

maybe Wáng Wéi
would have painted that,

but he did not paint anything
like our fires

though he would have understood them, though he might
have smelled them

grinding his ink stick
against water.

The Motion Picture Retirement Home, Two East: What Is She Reading?

What is she reading? Still reading
the biography of Esther Williams
who used to live down the street
and invited them for drinks
although they were not movie people, really.
Her husband sold drapes
to the studios, but that was another story.
Esther invited them for drinks anyway.

So what is she asking for? Juice,
she just had juice, but she hasn't
had juice in years, at least not
in those nice cut crystal goblets
that replaced the jelly jar collection
after the children grew up enough
to hold a good glass in their hands
without dropping it.

Her daughter comes with crystal necklaces
on the weekend and leaves them
with her. She used to twine them
around her wrists in the style
of Esther Williams. Such a nice woman
Miss Williams was, invited them to parties many times.
What was Esther Williams thinking? That her husband
could redo the drapes for nothing? That they were rich
enough living in Bel Air, too, almost next door, so why not?

La Brea

*The La Brea Tar Pits (or Rancho La Brea Tar Pits) are a cluster
of tar pits around which Hancock Park was formed in the urban heart
of Los Angeles. Asphaltum or tar ("brea" in Spanish) has seeped up
from the ground in this area for tens of thousands of years. The tar is
often covered with water. Over many centuries, animals that came
to drink the water fell in, sank in the tar, and were preserved as bones.*
—from Wikipedia

Awake in the night, pain
I know the places of.
Long bones and short
and their intersections with muscle and tendon.

I lie there imagining the shapes
of sockets and hinges
and the lines of ligaments,
the toll roads I ride and pay for.

There's a pile of X-rays and MRIs
under the coffee table in my workroom.
Me and the dogs—our bones,
our ghostly and beautiful spines in a heap.

We're settling, we're going down
together in the shadowy tar around our images,
la brea, the ever moving tar,
the bone sink and churner.

We're going down, unarticulated,
indistinguishable then. All the old dogs going down,
greyly illuminated, our bones shining
and sleeker than we knew.

WHAT MARRIES YOU

for Keith and John

The old man of the moon, also known as Jie Lín, the God of Marriage, is said to decide the mystical union of mortals and record them in a book; he is also believed to connect their feet with an invisible red silk thread.

What marries you is
the thin red line at the rim
of the morning before you
open your eyes to it,
and then the kitchen and the coffee
and the papers on the table.

The table set for two
marries you,
the arrangement of cups,
the pattern of glasses and plates,
what you put away in the cupboard
marries you.

What marries you carries
through the day, your common desires
and the concert of needs
written to their music.

Your wedding is all the trips to the store
and the phone calls,
and a gift of flowers
for no special reason—
and performing the flowers,
you are a blossom
in the vase of his love.

What marries you are the feelings
you talk about and don't hold away.
Sadness marries you, and deaths
you must witness, the length of loss
and the sharp corners of grief.

Falling asleep, whatever the watery dark
inhabits of you, each is marrying the other
there, wanting to wake again
to that world with him in it above all.

Awash in time, time marries you.
Each hour is an hour
you fill in his lifetime,
each moment you are his heartbeat's measure.

There was not one day more than another.
Each day marrying each other,
the thin red string between you, fastening.

And here you are—marrying still and married,
showing the steps danced so long together,
showing the turns of that vulnerable music
that has been carrying you on.

What marries you stands before you
for all to see.

Escucha, Mi Vida

Listen, my life!

You were a leaf
on a cecropia,
a breathing leaf,
a sun shield,
a daughter of the branch,
of the trunk,
of the root.

A Blue-grey Tanager
pushed you aside
for the fruit.
The wind pushed you,
the afternoon rain
bent you low.

Listen, my life.
When you went falling
against a backdrop of blue sky,
a brown curl
loose in the air,
you were done with that lifetime on a stem.

Done with the green breath
you went, down
to the surging current.
You were a new boat
moving between
the dark stones
and the light stones,
finding the open "V" and sailing
across the swell.

My life, I saw you go by
from the freshly painted
green bridge
over the beautiful *quebrada*
when I had stepped newly born
from the forest
into a patch of sun.

This Next Attempt Will Be Meta-poetical

because the metaphorical material of my situation
kept presenting itself as too obviously & unbelievably facile
even after I had taken my poem through five drafts
and mentally carried it on several walks along the river.
I told my friend Tara that no one would believe I hadn't
just made up a narrative to produce such perfect metaphors.
The original poem in several versions was high on my playlist
from all that walking but not one of them was carrying
the right kind of tune and it was or was not a love poem
though it covers the time we thought we would break up
and went to therapy to see if we should or how to do it
if we should or if there was a way to go on,

and while this was happening we were also in the design stages,
of a major remodel of our house because we needed more usable space and
the space designer had some ideas that shook not only the foundation but
us, so there was that tension as well, but we had learned
from past remodeling ventures that it was best for us to stay
on the same side and up against the contractor or the carpenter
or tile setter or whatever because that way they can't
divide and conquer you right in the shambles
of the earthquake wrecked fireplace and ignite a pile
of accumulating interests or kick around some still living embers
of indecision on our parts or tensions between us
passing as indecision or amazement at the costs,
and so they could get a pretty good blaze going
allowing them to make the best case to do what they wanted
to do to the floor or the walls or countertop and we two smolder
for the rest of the day and they get away with their plans
and we argue over dinner at that bistro where everyone knows us
as gals from the neighborhood but they don't recognize
this "not speaking" or the stilted conversation or

one or the other tearing up or downright crying
into the cloth napkin.

So, there's remodeling a house as metaphor
for emotional upheaval with a good end in sight
but going to therapy for the first time ever in 22 years
as a potential high-stakes deal breaker discussion.

Then there's the letter from the city saying that
some time in the next few months our street
will be closed at both ends because the entire length
of it is going to be peeled off and new asphalt poured
and the letter can't get more specific than that though
soon enough signs appear on the poles up and down
the street saying the same vague things until one day
it is true enough and the city trucks roll in and guys
sit around for awhile while waiting for the boss and
the people from the Gas Company and the Department
of Water and Power to locate all the "no-no zones"
so that nothing gets out of hand and then fire burst out
all up and down the block or power outages screw up
the "work from home" folks or the screenwriters
who frequent the Starbucks at the end of the street (the one
we secretly wish would go up in smoke).

The road, the path, the way in, the way out, created the multi-layered
meaning that really made my first idea for the poem
too incredibly easy to write even though all of it was true
because here we are talking about splitting up while
remodeling our house and waiting for the street
to be fixed so it's a smooth thoroughfare again
only this time there will be speed bumps because

the coffee junkies speed down the block as if the last
cup of coffee on earth is about to be sold to the person
in front of them in line and that's why they can't park
in the parking lot but must jockey to get one of the six
metered parking spots within fifty feet of the door.

What they must have been feeling is probably close to what we
were feeling so I shouldn't make light of the plight of those addicts
but should remember how edgy anything can get when
everything is riding on that one hot shot of an answer
to a completely fucked situation, how meaningful, how
unbearably obvious and meaningful any real thing can be
in the midst of what you never thought could happen to you again.

WHAT DOES DEATH WANT FROM ME?

Just hanging around,
picking up something from the table, say, a bill

or the insurance form half-filled in,
or the map of New Mexico or the bird book.

Just looking,
not saying much,

like people who draw attention
to themselves by being noisy with their silence.

Death already has the best part,
mom and dad and my dogs.

So, Death is shopping me now,
a regular used book addict

looking for that first edition by an author
nobody talks about anymore.

American *Jisei*

*The Japanese death poem, or jisei, is traditionally written
by monks and haiku poets immediately before their deaths.*

When I was most depressed,

> This is the "death poem," or *jisei*

certain scenarios would play in my head.

> of a Japanese poet named Kaisho.

I would imagine picking some unincorporated tract

> Although the consciousness of death is

in the high desert where gravel roads tail out

> in most cultures very much a part of life,

into sand, where it would take

> this is perhaps nowhere more true than in Japan,

months to find a body

> where the approach of death

deep in a tangle of creosote bushes

> has given rise to a centuries-old tradition

or propped against a Joshua Tree

> of writing such a poem,

A suicide note would be a luxury

often at the very moment

I could not afford myself, a small poem maybe.

the poet is breathing his last.

Note: The ten lines interwoven into "American Jisei" *are quoted from the front jacket flap of* Japanese Death Poems, *compiled by Yoel Hoffmann (Charles E. Tuttle Company, 1986)*

SPITBALL

for Mark Cull

Physicists speculate that when you leave a place,
a party, say, there are at least two universes where you go.
In one scenario, for example, you're a dog groomer.
In another, a free-agent spitball pitcher
who has gone back to Wichita to visit your family, circa 1982.
Neither of you returns to the party. Those two roads diverged
and kept on diverging. One's a north-south polar orbit
for a military satellite and one's the busiest freeway interchange
in the United States, a sweeping wing of rebar and concrete
hurling vehicles along a wicked curve toward LAX.

In either case, the party scene is basically over
for you. How many parties can one person
experience in this universe and any other ones?
How many pieces of celery can a single hand drag-bunt
across infinite varieties of soulfully flavored dip mixtures?
Wherever you are, it's time you go outside
for a breath of fresh air. There's a lingering whiff
of clover, and across the street from the party
some scruffy Standard Poodles are chasing each other
in an Astro-turfed yard. Your moistened fingertips
find the car key in the pocket of your dog-hair dusted coat.

Nobody is going to miss you if you go.

AND HAVING BROKEN INTO BLOSSOM

after James Wright

there is no against

just to and fro

and where before I wondered

what and why   now

I shyly bend and blend

into the sensible breeze

if there were anything

more to say

this pink of pink of pink

that I am

would be answer

enough

TRUE LOVE

for Maxine Kumin

Sometimes when Colleen and I wake up in the morning,
before we even get out of bed,
we say a few things about the day
and anticipate the newspaper headlines.

And then we talk about the baseball game.
Baseball's what's right with the world,
and good game or bad, there's something
to say about it.

We love the whole vocabulary of action
and the encyclopedic litany of measurement—
sixty feet six inches from pitcher to hitter,
fields as small as bandstands or spacious as national parks.

And then there's the speculative fiction
of how our pitching will hold up against really heavy hitters,
the kind from the Midwest whose statistics are beefy,
or East Coast lineups whose averages soar like skyscrapers.

If home runs could inscribe the air,
last night's fusillade would hang there,
a neon arcade of arching and ethereal trails
backed up by palm trees and headlights in the parking lots

that ring Dodger Stadium,
itself a stack of circles,
and nothing at all like the flat courts of the Aztecs
where "play ball" was a death sentence.

Much better here where there's always a tomorrow,
a clean score sheet waiting for its statistical narrative
to unfold among greasy popcorn fingerprints
and cotton candy smears in rainbow colors.

Who can't love the "pandemaniacal" anthems of the crowd,
the beach balls bounding from the outfield pavilions,
the improbable and impossible overlap
of diamonds and circles and squares all in play?

It's enough to get you out of bed in the morning
and, like Max, get all your poetry written
before the first pitch of the day is thrown.

Index of Poems

Biographical Note

Eloise Klein Healy is the author of seven books of poetry and three spoken word recordings. She was the founding chair of the MFA in Creative Writing Program at Antioch University Los Angeles where she is Distinguished Professor of Creative Writing Emerita. Healy directed the Women's Studies Program at California State University Northridge and taught in the Feminist Studio Workshop at The Woman's Building in Los Angeles. She is the founding editor of Arktoi Books, an imprint of Red Hen Press specializing in the work of lesbian authors. In December 2012, Healy was appointed the first Poet Laureate of The City of Los Angeles.

Healy was born in El Paso, Texas, and spent her childhood in Remsen, Iowa, before moving with her family to North Hollywood, California. She attended Providence High School, Immaculate Heart College, and Vermont College. She currently lives in Sherman Oaks, California, with Colleen Rooney and their dog, Nikita.